IN THEIR OWN WORDS

Rising from the Ashes of the Sonoma County Wildfires.

by: Paul Holbrook

In Their Own Words Publishing

4622 Runabout Way Bradenton FL. 34203

941-799-4807

Special thanks to everyone who opened their hearts to tell their story. Thank you for giving me permission to share your story with the world. I know this was not easy. Our thoughts and prayers are with each of you.

When I left that night to pick my son up from the airport, all was quiet. By the time I got back, all hell had broken loose.

Nothing could have prepared me for what was happening and what would come.

I've been through fires before. Earthquakes. Train crashes. Community tragedies. But I've never been through anything quite like the Sonoma County fires.

Some might say they tore the city apart. Others might say they brought it together. All I know for sure is that I've never in my life felt more heart, love and strength than I did in the aftermath of that devastation. There's a reason why, "The Love in the Air Is Thicker Than the Smoke" became the motto for the community and surrounding cities. It's because that's how it felt to live there. We were instantly connected. And we still are.

This book is an example of that. The stories included are ones of triumph, heartbreak, hope and perseverance. Paul has done a fantastic job bringing people together to talk about a difficult chapter in their lives. He wanted their stories to be told in their own words. I commend him for doing just that and I hope you enjoy his work.

Jenn Sterling

New York Times Bestselling Author

& Petaluma Resident

FORWARD

I was not in Santa Rosa when the Tubbs fire occurred in October of 2017. I arrived in March of 2018. My wife, an RN, was working a travel assignment at one of the hospitals there. We were staying at the Extended Stay America located at the entrance to Fountain Grove subdivision. Those of you who know the area are aware that this hotel is located across the street from the iconic Round Barn. At least, the Round Barn used to be there….

The devastation I saw during my time in Santa Rosa was indescribable. The city saw a population decrease of 20,000, as residents had no choice but to relocate to other cities and other states. Homes and histories went up in flames, so did the hopes of thousands.

Included in that number were many surgeons who practiced at the hospital where my wife worked.   Some had already left town. The few that stayed were concerned about the stories being conveyed in the news. One doctor told my wife that the stories were not being reported truthfully. "That's not the way it happened", he said, "I wish people here had a way to tell the real story!"

I was intrigued with the idea. I had no idea if the people were ready to tell what they saw that night. I thought it may be too soon, and the horrors were still too fresh to communicate. Our hotel was filled with workers who were rebuilding the town, and most of them had not seen the fire firsthand. So, they could not tell me anything. However, when I spoke to the hotel staff, I could tell the PTSD was real and it was deeply rooted. Some thought the book was a good idea and others thought I should not touch the subject. I was not sure if the residents affected would even talk to me: someone who came to town after the fact. But, after hearing the doctor's lament, I took to Facebook to find out if Santa Rosans were interested in sending me letters to tell their story.

The response was overwhelming. People needed an outlet to tell what happened to them personally. They poured out their replays of the firestorm that made history. You could feel the emotions they felt in all of the letters.

That is how this book was born: to give the residents a chance to tell their experiences in their own words. There are stories of heroism and horror. There are near misses and folks who lost everything. There are stories of people who barely got out, and people who rushed back in to help those in need.

I had to choke back the tears as I read each one. Some people promised to send their story only to text me back saying that they could not write it yet: The trauma was too fresh.

I did not edit the stories that came in. The words, sentence structures, and all the emotions are original. Trying to polish it would have taken the guts out of a story that will live in their hearts forever. You will read the REAL horror and tears that these precious people tried to pour out on paper. Never have I been so moved by anything I have read. So, grab a box of tissues before you begin.... you will need it.

I will not add any more commentary. I wanted to give them a chance to tell the story in their own words. Here are their tales.......

Paul Holbrook

Robert Morgan

From: Robert Morgan

Sent: Wednesday, February 21, 2018 2:07 PM

To: Aaron Mix

subject: North Bay wildfire/journeys end mobile home park

Good day to you sir. Although the early morning of October 8th seems still so fresh in my mind and emotions, it has been four months since that fire raced through Sonoma County and left in its wake record-breaking devastation.

I lived on Sahara Street – the last row of homes in the park. I awoke at 3:00 AM to find my bedroom filled with the kind of smoke one doesn't normally wake up from. Drunk by the smoke my head wouldn't clear. I drove a car to Kaiser, parked, and ran back to see what I can do. I ran down the dirt road behind my street that separated us from Kaiser, and I begin to address the firefighter standing by the engines. When a loud call came over the radios "EVACUATE KAISER! EVACUATE KAISER IMMEDIATELY!" Two of your men looked at me and kind of shrugged their shoulders. I identified myself as a former firefighter and yelled out "if you can't do it at least give me a firehose and let me try" and they did.

You showed up a few minutes later, followed the hose out to me and said, "what are you doing?". And I yelled back, "trying to save my F ing Street!". You looked to your left and to your right, saw how many homes were still unburned and you said very clearly, "we can do that".

It was dark, the only light being provided by the fire. I couldn't see your face, but I will never forget your words as long as I live. And the next thing I knew, you sent three of your finest to help save those homes! And talk about bad ass firefighters, those guys spaced themselves out and with 65 mph winds, smoke, injures and debris in the face for three hours – they stood in the middle of that street and kept that fire from reaching the homes behind them. By the time it became light out, we could see the carnage the fire left in the park – it looked like London after the blitz. While they were beating back the flames on their end of the street, I was working on mine.

I was joined by an unsung hero named Steve, whose dad lived a few doors down from me, on oxygen. He came out of nowhere. I ask if his Dad got out, and he said yes! And I asked myself why the hell did he come back here? Nobody returns to an inferno. He was helping me with the hose when he heard what he thought was a dog barking. I yelled out that everybody had been evacuated, nobody would leave their dog. And we went back to work. But again, he insisted he heard a dog barking, so I looked up the street and the only dog between us was my neighbors. So, we went up to her house, and sure enough, I could see her little one-pound dog barking in the left-hand corner of the glass sliding door.

However, as I looked to my right, I saw feet, legs, knees and wheelchair wheels. It was my neighbor, Martha Sue Sinnott. Her mouth was closed, but her eyes were screaming a deafening scream. We opened her door and she yelled out, "they left me". From where she was sitting in her wheelchair, she could see the Fountain Grove Hilton fully involved and 30-foot flames reaching for the stars and coming her way. She believed she was all alone and going to burn to death with her dog.

I ran and found you, and you sent some big burly guys and they carried her to safety. As long as I live I will see her face. She passed January 11, from heart issues I believe were born of that fire. Footnote: there is NO WAY Steve could have heard that dog, as far away as we were, with ALL the noise, wind, gas main out-front blowing like a jet engine – God put the sound of that dog in Steve's ear and made sure we got that woman out of her house. There were many miracles that morning and in the days that followed.

When it was all over, thanks to those first two who gave me the hose, and thanks to you for throwing those 3 Firefighters My Way, together we were able to save 43 homes from burning to the ground, and one wheelchair-bound grandma lady's life! My place was condemned by my insurance company, so I was homeless for a while but found a temporary place for now. Things are beginning to slow down, I wanted to reach out to you, and your men that worked the Journey's End Fire. I have been working on a 'heartfelt thank you' kind of thing but realized I don't know their names. Could you please allow me to have their names, so I can finish up what I've been working on? I would then like to meet with all of you to pay my respects and show my gratitude, as well as those whose homes they saved. All of you have done so much and we want to have the opportunity to properly thank all of you. Please, I hope this is your right email address, please let me know if you get this.

Thank you,

Priest Morgan, formerly of 448 Sahara St., Journey's End.

You guys rock!!!

Jason Jenkins

From: Jason Jenkins

To: Aaron Mix

February 23, 2018

Aaron, Robert,

Aaron – Thanks for passing this along. I added Robert to the reply and hope he gets this.

I would like to thank both of you for your amazing work that night. I could not have said it any better that what was just described. When I first arrived at the park, I tried to enter off Mendocino and was pushed back by multiple explosions and fire.

I ran into Robert a bit later at the rear of Kaiser. At that time, I had no engines. Luckily, you showed and took on the challenge. As my focus was on the Kaiser Evacuation, part of that plan of success heavily relied on your guys efforts to hold that last row of home on Sahara Street.

I was very impressed with both your abilities and willingness to battle: no matter what the setback.

Take care, and don't hesitate to reach out.

Thanks,

Jason Jenkins, Battalion Chief

Santa Rosa FD

Marilyn Glynn

It was in the early morning hours of October 9, 2017, that changed our life completely. This is our story...

Sometime before 2 a.m., I woke up to lots of commotion outside...emergency lights flashing and over a loud-speaker "Get out now." Being half-asleep and not comprehending what was going on, I thought it was a drug raid going down in our neighborhood. As I listened more carefully to the voice over the loud-speaker, I realized he was saying "Evacuate now. This is an emergency. You must leave now." Looking out the window, I saw our neighbors fleeing in their cars. I woke up my husband and we threw on our clothes from the night before. Our power was out so our house was in total darkness.

My husband grabbed a flashlight and retrieved the cat carriers from the rafters in the garage. I managed to get Stuart right away. Max, scared by all the commotion, was nowhere to be found. We looked under beds, moved couches thinking he might be behind or under them. Finally, my husband found Max, frozen with fear, under a bed. He hurriedly stuffed Max in the cat carrier.

So, we left. I grabbed my purse, ring, watch and iPhone, oh, and some money I had in my underwear drawer. We left behind everything else...the back-up drive to the computer, all our photo albums of our life together, my memoir, family heirlooms...everything material that told a story of our life.

We left in the darkness by the side door in the garage. My husband locked it, so the contents would be safe for when we were able to return. We still, at that moment, did not know our house would be consumed by flames from the firestorm.

As we left, the wind was fiercely swirling tons of leaves and debris from our neighbor's trees behind us. My husband's thought was "Damn, I have a big mess to clean up when we return." "When we return".... there was no returning to what was. It was so smokey, you could barely see. The wind had to be blowing 60 miles an hour. As we drove away, I remembered Maynard, our turtle, outside in his pond. There was no turning back.

Not knowing where to go, we left our Larkfield home and drove towards Airport Blvd. Parked alongside the road, we could see the red glow of the fire in the distance. Occasionally we could see a tree burst into flames. The sound of propane tanks and gas mains boomed through the air.

We were finally allowed back on our property several weeks later. We found Maynard, who perished in the fire in his outside pond. Just about everything was reduced to ash. There was nothing left to show of our life. It was as though we never existed...

Allison Glynn-Wilson

Mom, this brings tears to my eyes. We have had a heartbreaking year and you and Dad have been so strong. Every day is a sad discovery of a memory or lost item from your lives, my life, our lives. Your home of 42 years and the accumulation of 75 years of living is gone. But you and Dad exist. Your lives exist. A fire cannot take that away even if it seems like the whole world has forsaken you.

We have a "new normal." And it hurts, and it sucks, and it isn't fair. Fuck. It shouldn't be this way. Everything you and Dad worked your entire lives for is now gone. You should be living your retirement free and easy, enjoying the beautiful space you two created.

I remember messaging you that night when we found out about the fire. You told me that in your heart of hearts you knew the House was gone. Dad held out hope. When I finally saw a picture that a neighbor posted of our home, it hit me like a punch in the gut. I had to

show you and Dad the picture to confirm what our worst fear was.

When we were able to go back to the property, it was surreal, heartbreakingly unreal. Your reaction when we found Maynard will stick with me always. The defeat on Dad's face and in his body is something that will always tear me up inside. Small pieces of things became treasures even if it was a piece of tarnished silverware from Grandma's set or a broken piece of Corning ware or a broken piece of a pinch pot I made as a child or a broken piece of a pot that held flowers. Broken pieces. An entire life evaporated except for broken pieces.

But you have raised a good family and every memory is something we still retain. Any old picture a friend sends is cherished. Any traditions still remain with modifications. You may have "downsized", but I am in awe of the perseverance that you and Dad have. I learned from you as a child in our Brighton Ct. home and I still continue to learn from you in its absence.

I love you.

Allison Glynn-Wilson

Marilyn Glynn

Now you have brought me to tears. ♡ I know that losing our home has been devastating to you as well. This is where you grew up and where you created memories of your own. With your strength and support, dad and I will get through this. We have already made "modified" memories...an Easter Egg hunt on our barren property and, on Christmas, making a toast to better times ahead by sipping champagne and smashing our wine glasses to where our fireplace used to be. Love you, mom

Craig Schwartz

There are many stories to tell from the morning of October 9. Tales of tragedy and heroism, lives lost and many more lives saved. I can tell you that working in the City's emergency operations center to evacuate residents that night was the scariest night of my career. I was in no danger there but listening to the Santa Rosa Police Officers' radio traffic about the rescues they were carrying out in Fountaingrove, Skyfarm, Journey's End Mobile Home Park, Coffey Park, and elsewhere had me convinced that the loss of life that night would be extreme.

The heroism on display from police officers, firefighters, sheriff's deputies, bus drivers, residents, and many others was amazing to witness. I believe it is because of these extraordinary efforts that so many were saved. We want to bring you some of the stories of that night, and this first recounting brings you just a small portion of the events of October 8 and 9.

Officer Andy Adams is a Santa Rosa patrol officer who was working swing shift the night of the fires and began evacuating people from the area of Skyfarm and St. Andrews Drive at about 11:30 pm. As he tells it, the fire moved so quickly that it engulfed the area where he and Officer Eric St. Germain were driving. As they worked to evacuate residents they found a woman who lived in the 3900 block of St. Andrews Drive, trying to escape the firestorm. They told her to follow them out by driving her car between the two patrol cars. The fire was blowing across the road in their path however, and they had to turn around. The smoke was so thick that it was nearly impossible to see, and the woman ran into the curb on one side of the road., and then the other. Officer Adams passed her and led the way out by driving with the reflective centerline markers between his tires. Even then, a burning tree had fallen across the road and almost prevented their escape. The two officers got the woman out of harm's way, then went back into the fire to rescue more people.

In the 3700 block of Skyfarm Drive, Officer Adams and Officer Dave Pedersen found several people at a house down a long driveway. The first man they encountered there said he couldn't get out, so they told him to get in Officer Pedersen's car. The man also said his family was inside but couldn't get out because the power was out, and the garage door wouldn't open. Officer Adams ran in the house, popped the emergency release on the door and opened it so the family could escape in their own car. The officers continued their work and evacuated residents from the Hopper Lane Apartments and Coffey Park once the fire had jumped Highway 101. At one home on Keoke Court, Officer Adams, Officer St. Germain and others carried a number of wheelchair-bound elderly residents to their patrol cars as "fire whirls" or tornados of burning embers blew around them. Near the end of what would have been Officer Adams' twelve and a half hour shift his radio battery died and he had to go back to the police department for a replacement, where he met up with Sergeant Pehlke.

Sgt. Pehlke was not supposed to work that night but came in at about 3 am when he got the call about the firestorm. He met Officer Adams at the police department and since Patrol cars were getting scarce they paired up to rescue more people.

Their first call together was to the Varenna Senior Living Apartments. As they drove up Fountaingrove Parkway, the fire had burned many of the buildings in the area and was burning within feet of the road. They had to dodge burning trees that had blown down in the heavy winds and blocked the road. When they got to Varenna they found a woman trying to evacuate her mother from a building that was already on fire. They found dozens of elderly residents in the lobby of the smoke-filled building, and along with other officers checked the building for any other people. The heroic woman they had encountered loaded 4-5 of the residents into her car, while Sgt. Pehlke and Officer Adams were able to get more officers and city buses there to evacuate the rest of the residents.

After completing those rescues, they had to help rescue an elderly woman who was trapped in a motel room near the bottom of Fountaingrove Parkway, and then were sent back to Varenna and eventually to an address on Tall Pine Circle. A woman had called 911 to say she had evacuated her house there, but her husband was trapped and that the house was on fire. Sgt. Pehlke and Officer Adams found the whole neighborhood engulfed in flames, with fire a mere three to four feet from their patrol car as they drove in. They got to the house in question and although all the houses around it were burning, it had not yet caught fire. They found the elderly man in his bedroom and walked him to their patrol car as burning embers blew all around them. Sgt. Pehlke saw the man had no clothes, so he ran back into the house and grabbed some clothing as well as several pictures hanging on the walls.

The three fled the house, driving through the blowing embers and fire to deliver the man safely at the Veteran's Memorial Building shelter before they drove back into Fountaingrove to conduct more rescues. As they drove up the hill from Brush Creek Road though, they smelled the odor of burning rubber and saw smoke pouring through the air vents on their dashboard. Sgt. Pehlke made a quick U-turn to get out of the fire zone and then saw flames licking up at his feet from the floor of the car. They got to the bottom of the hill and jumped out of the car, quickly grabbing the computer, rifle and shotgun before it was completely engulfed in flames.

Even though their car burned, their work continued, and they were quickly back out in a different vehicle to continue the evacuations. The picture shown here is the patrol car they had been driving shortly after they got out. This is the kind of extraordinary work that we saw over and over during the fires of October. We look forward to sharing more of them with you and invite you to share your stories with us. As Chief Schreeder has said, everyone was a first responder that night, and people looking out for their friends, family, and neighbors showed incredible selflessness and heroism. Their stories should be told as well.

Thank you for reading. - Craig Schwartz

Bobbi N Sean Donovan

October 20, 2017 · Healdsburg ·

So many people have said "I can't imagine how you feel". Honestly, I don't know how I feel. Most of the time it's gratitude. When it's anything else, I feel stunned and uncertain. "I don't know" literally comes out of my mouth 800 times a day. For those who know me, that is out of my comfort zone.

We are doing ok. Sean and I look like walking zombies. The girls have been spending some much-needed time with their village while Sean and I return to work. Work that is constantly interrupted with trying to find a home messages and calls. (Thank you, Bob Austin, Skye Woodward & Kevin Crosbie for the grace to just do the best we can right now.)

Any homes that you know of-please let us know. (Thank you Shannon Schiller) I think you have amazing skill at house hunting!!) We are following up on all of them. Too bad the rehome group didn't in the first days when there were houses.

Looks like we are moving again tomorrow. Oh, how we will miss the HH and the nice lady Fatima (who ALWAYS has a smile) that we say "good night. See you tomorrow!" to.

Having breakfast made and served with such warm smiles and all of the luxury here has been amazing. The next three years will be anything BUT luxurious. We will be moving to a place that will provide a kitchen, a shower, two rooms for space to retreat when we need, and a way for Sean and me to sleep next to each other again. I never thought I'd admit this-but I miss kicking him because he is snoring too loud! Hershey, too. He has been in one room with the dogs and one kid. I've been in another with two kids.

FEMA announced they plan to have clean up done and begin rebuilding mid-January. I'm glad-mostly. They are of scoop up our lives and toss them in the trash-potentially including some missing loved ones. I can't wrap my mind around that. The rain makes me feel the same way-it's needed for the fire, but I want every single missing body, and anything left that can be used to conclusively identify them preserved. I think we need that closure.

Thank you all for wrapping your arms around us and so many of our friends who are in our shoes. Your generosity and tireless effort to check on us is immeasurable. We are working on storage, so we can say "yes" to the many offers of "things" we lost. We are gonna work on taking over part of the garage at Judy Hutton's and storing stuff that won't fit in the van.

Thank you is so small. But that's all we have to offer. Thank you.

The Traveling Donovans

Bobbi N Sean Donovan

November 5, 2017 ·

It just occurred to me that 4 Sundays ago right about now Sean sat down to watch the news, just as he did tonight. Only that night I begged him not to go to bed because the power had been flickering and the air was smokey. He went anyway. I stayed up attempting to study for my midterm the following day. I was so giddy to get to spend the day with our entire Redwood CU family at the LBC for a day of inspiration. Who knew how inspiring that day would ultimately come to be.

I feel like I should be walking around like a zombie all lifeless and dazed. Not to say that I didn't feel completely STUNNED a few times the first few days after the fire.

I don't feel lost. I truly feel like we have gained so much in spite of all that we lost. We have had more family and friend time together, we have had more meals together (with our hectic schedules that's hard to do), we've had more fun, we have had more opportunities to say thank you's to loved ones and friends we hadn't even met yet, we have had more hugs, more I love you's, more patience with each other, more kindness in our entire universe, I feel more hopeful that those home repairs we always put off will finally get done, I'm more proud than ever of my kids (2 and 4 legged) for their resiliency, I'm more in awe of Sean and more thankful that he asked me to be his bride-ok, maybe it was my idea-but it was a good choice! I'm more confident that I, too resilient, ABLE, resourceful, discerning, loved and cherished. I have been truly living a peace that passes all understanding. It's all kind of liberating.

More than anything, I see reminders every day, everywhere that now is the time to call on my faith and trust that He will continue to bring beauty from ashes and strength from fears. Feel free to sing along.

https://youtu.be/hEDvSFGZt9I

My prayers are with those trapped in grief. I'm here for those who need a pick up or a friend to celebrate our victories. I'm so pleased that most of us have secured a place to live while we rebuild. 🙏

#thisaintnosprintrace #faithfirst

#sonomastrong #blessed

#thankyouforyourkindness

I'll compose a short story and share ASAP. It will help to write about it. Feel free to look back on my wall in the weeks immediately following the event. I was pretty good at sharing raw emotions.

Conversation between Bobbi N Sean Donovan and Paul Holbrook,

Rising from the Ashes administrator

Thank you so much. It is an amazing story. I went through an individual house fire about 6 years ago.

Bobbi N Sean

I'm so sorry. How are you now? I imagine life 6 years post. I think we'll be fine, but never the same.

Rising from the Ashes

Yes, we are doing great now. I remember getting the call from my wife while I was at work saying the house was on fire. It was hard to figure out what to do the first week, but the Red Cross paid for a hotel room for us. The biggest thing we learned was that things are just things. Apart from pictures and a few keepsakes, we don't miss many of the things we thought were so dear to us.

Rising from the Ashes

You are right: fine but never the same.

Bobbi N Sean

I was fortunate that we had put the wedding negatives in a safe deposit box. We forgot that we had. It was funny, I thought had accepted that they were gone. Forever. But, I was still too nervous to look. If I looked and they were not there-they were TRULY gone forever. But what if they were there? THEY WERE!!! I ugly cried right there in the bank!

Bobbi N Sean

I think it's easier to be a part of such a massive amount of despair and loss vs a single home loss. There's an unspoken "sisterhood" feeling in our lives. I'm so sorry for your loss. Our hardest part was the 18 pets.

Jun 18th, 2:46pm

Rising from the Ashes

So sorry about the pets. Our pets spent a night in oxygen tents after the fire. I can't imagine finding a place to live after your fire. With the single house fire, we were able to check into the first hotel we went to. With that many people homeless, I am sure that was hard to find a place. Thank you for your contribution.

Bobbi N Sean

We moved several times. Ultimately, we ended up on the SAME street we left to move into the house that burned down. It's pretty bittersweet. We are back playing at the park where we first pushed our kids on swings, back where the old chocolate lab, Hershey played as a puppy. He's aged a ton through this and may not make it home again. What's really great is this house became available because my landlords, who lived there even when we lived on that street years ago, had split up. She moved into a home she inherited through the loss of a family member two years ago. The fire helped them realize there's still a lot of love between them and they needed to work on their marriage. He took the tenant with them that was at our house and moved in with the wife. The tenant has since moved home to San Diego and made amends with estranged family members.
The house had a full kitchen, some furniture, TVs, and PETS! There are koi and turtles. Super exciting, the koi just made babies. We are proud new parents of a koi fry. ♥ this is

great for us because we had a lot of critters who needed bugs. We used to live basically in a biology classroom with all the breeding we did!

Fortunately, we saved the two dogs and the guinea pig.

I'm glad you are all ok!

Gretchen Van Tassel

Something really bad happened last October 2017. There were bad sudden wildfires! It started late eve of Oct 8th and these fires spread all over the area of Santa Rosa And in to Sonoma valley. I had started smelling smoke in later evening I went outside, and the smoke smell was getting a stronger and I was now worried, where was the fire?

I finally turned onto the news and the first announcement was a fire in Napa county. I wondered why? Because the smell of smoke was getting more and more serious. So, then I finally heard of a fire in the area of Calistoga. So, I knew this was what I was smelling.

I noticed that it was really windy outside! So, then I knew the fires were coming fast!! I then was wondering, And I felt really worried that what if a fire gotten close to Hood Mtn! Because it's my special place.

My friend Wayne was here with me I had asked him to come over to keep me company because I was getting really scared about the fires!

Then I was outside, and I saw that the smoke was getting a very thick and it had almost covered up the moon! So, it was really, really bad! I saw some of my neighbors and they were wondering about all the smoke and I told them the news of the fires. Then, I finally decided about planning to evacuate because this fire, I knew was getting closer and closer to the area where I live on Range and Russell Ave. This is near Codding town.

I was thinking about what to take with me. So, I packed my medicine and got some important pictures together. I also grabbed up my birth certificate and high school diploma. I thought about getting a bag of clothes, but I was starting to get very nervous and panic. Then also I have 2 cats and I got the carriers ready to load them up.

Then I was thinking about who going to takes me to somewhere safe, so I called my friend Jody who lives right next to me and asked her, but she thought the fire wasn't that serious, but I told her it was. Also, I told my friend Wayne that he's should get someone to take him as well. Then I called my friend Jimmy and he said that him and his girlfriend were getting ready to leave Oakmont where they were living.

So, then I had found out from Jimmy that there was a fire coming over in Sonoma Valley. So, then I got so, so worried that the fires might spread onto Hood Mtn! So, I finally heard on the news that the fires had gone over to mark west springs area!

So, then I heard that the fire had jumped across highway 101!! That confirmed my worst fears that it so really close now! I had always wondered if a fire could jump over the freeway. But it sure did this time! I knew it was getting really close to where I live, and I got real scared now!

Then I heard the news caster say on TV that everyone in the area where the fires were coming should evacuate now! Asap. So, then I called my mom and told her there was a bad fire coming and if I could have someone get me over to her place in Sebastopol and as far as knew there was no fires there. My mom had been asleep and didn't know of the fires and she say ok for me to come So I called Jody and she said that she can take both me and Wayne.

But then I went outside, and I saw smoke so much and couldn't see the moon because the sky all filled up of smoke. Then I heard sounds booms and popping noises like some buildings were going up in flames! I wondered if it were a store nearby or a house!

So also, I finally saw sparks and embers flying over my apt! I knew I had to get out of here fast! Then I was about to get ready to go meet Jody, but I still hadn't loaded up my cats yet and knew I had to. Then I was outside, and Jimmy and Kelly showed up and Jimmy asked Melissa if I was ok and then it was decided that I would go with Jimmy and Kelly. So, I got my stuff that I had ready to go and then I told Jimmy that I still had to get the cats, But Jimmy was honest that there was NO room for the cats!! well him and Kelly had lots of stuff plus 2 small dogs. So, I could see that it was already crowded in Kelly's car.

Well so very sadly I had to leave White socks and Tuxie behind! I was so sad! I knew others had leave their pet's behind if they couldn't find them.

So, then I went on the way to my moms and as we were driving thru town there was lots of traffic. Everyone was getting away from the fires path! I still worried about the fire getting Hood Mtn, but I just had to accept whatever was going to happen would happen. I thought hopefully if the fires spread in to my apt complex maybe my cats will survive somehow. Well I had left them inside.

Then I got to my moms and told her more on the fires and a neighbor of my mom's was out talking to us. My mom had thanked both Jimmy and Kelly for getting me over to her place.

Then I finally got settled down to sleep: I had stayed up really late. I hadn't got to my mom's till between 2 and 3 in morn of Oct 9th.

So then, later that day, I watched lots of news about all the fires. I was shocked couldn't believe how much destruction. Then I finally found out that my apartment complex was ok and so I knew my cats and all my stuff was ok but NOT a lot of other places were ok because lots homes and businesses got burned up!! I founded out that the k mart store was gone and McDonald's and Applebee's and Arby's all gone!! destroyed. Then this was really sad. The historic round barn burnt to the ground!

Well so I ended up staying at my mom for 1 week and couldn't go back to my place because the gas and power were turned off (I guess) because of the fires. Then on Oct 14 and 15 another fire flared up off Pythian rd. right at the bottom of Hood Mtn!! So, I was really upset!!

The last summer of 2017 I had a really bad nightmare of a dream about a fire on Hood Mtn! So now it came true! I just couldn't believe it! It was so real! Well I saw the news on TV and it showed live footage of Hood Mtn on fire!! I was really devastated, and I said "NO, NO" a few times and I think I was almost crying.

Well it was good thing my mom was out of the house because I kinda yelled and I picked up my mom's cat for comfort. Well so that was a very upsetting and hard times during the fires and I felt really bad for everyone who lost their homes and pets!

Well tragically about 40 people lost their lives in the fires. Then some other (of course) hills and mtns burned like Bennett Mtn and the ridge and part of Mt St. Helena and sugar loaf. But not Taylor Mtn or pretty much all of Sonoma Mtn was ok. So that's my fire story. SO, you can put it in the book with all my permission.

By Gretchen Van Tassel

Sasha Butler

Sunday, October 8th was picture perfect. Sunshine and warm winds. I hiked while my finance stayed home in Coffey Park and painted baseboards in the driveway, getting ready to finish up on his 10-month long remodeling project. He had meticulously installed all new kitchen cabinets and flooring. Every detail was considered, and we were both so proud of all the work he had done. We watched the 10 o'clock news as usual, seeing that there was a fire in Calistoga. As with most news stories about floods and fires we said how fortunate we were having his house in a subdivision, not near a river or forest - we were safe.

Fast forward to 1:30am. The burning in my nose from the smoke coming through the door woke me. I got up, looked outside and saw that there were large ashes blowing and it was smokey. I went back to the bedroom and shut the door, thinking the winds were blowing the smoke from Calistoga. Minutes later I start hearing loud explosions. It must be transformers being knocked out from the winds.

The last explosion I heard sounded like it was under the house, which got us both out of bed (the dogs meanwhile slept through all of this). I looked out the bedroom window which faced Hopper Avenue. I could see the tops of cars and a police car with its lights on, but no siren. Logically this would indicate something is very wrong, but it was not sinking in yet that we needed to turn the tv on, something to tell us what to do. I checked my emails and saw the alerts.

Fire moved down Mark West. Fire had jumped 101 at Kohls. I got dressed, threw a left-over stuffed bell pepper in my bag and put my dog on his leash. We are standing in the living room looking at each other, me saying I think we need to leave seeing cars backing out of driveways on Hemlock Street.

Then suddenly, an orange glow. It illuminated the whole living room like an explosion. It is our neighbors' front yard, it is on fire. I am seeing this happening out the front window, still talking to Kevin who has his back to the window, and I let him finish telling me that I am over-reacting and that we do not need to go anywhere. I remember saying very matter of factly, "Julies yard is on fire".

I run out the front door and dial 9-1-1 and get a busy signal. Her neighbor has a hose on it, and it is out now. As I am heading back inside Kevin said he was staying, that he had a fire extinguisher and he was going to hang out in case anything happened. In hindsight I understand now, neither of us had any idea what was happening. A grass fire maybe? I tell him I am leaving and tell him to please do the same, please.

As I back out of the driveway and head south on Hemlock a police car passes me, and I can barely make out him saying to leave. Leave Now. I stop, roll down my window and he did the same. I say, which way do I go? The smoke is too thick to see his face and the wind too loud to hear him so we both pull away from each other.

The street lights are casting a glow in the smoke, an eerie orange glow. It is haunting now realizing that the lights had recently been changed to the bright white LEDs. That glow was not from the street lights, but from a raging firestorm, barreling down on homes and undoing everything only a block away, apparently. I see behind me Kevin getting his dog in his truck.

As I get towards the end of Hemlock I am 5 or 6 cars deep, brake lights on. I feel my leg shaking and it will not let me hold down the brake pedal, so I put it in park. Kevin calls me. Maybe 10 cars behind me. He says, "I think I am going to lose my house, that willow tree was hanging on my roof". Meanwhile, he is seeing everything catching on fire around him, yet I am only ahead of him a bit, and I do not remember seeing any fire at all.

It dawns on me that as I am sitting here in traffic I have not seen a fire truck, heard one siren, nothing. They must be on it, fighting it on Hopper. What usually takes about 2 minutes to drive between his house and Piner Road took 40 minutes. We are both heading to my house in Petaluma and arrive about 3:30am.

His neighbor had sent him texts between when we left and when he got to my house. Fire, everything burning. I remember just saying, oh my God. Over and over again. Seeing Kevin sitting there in my house with the realization that everything, just like that, is gone.

Still, we had no idea that his entire neighborhood was gone. A few homes maybe, but not close to 1300 homes just in Coffey Park alone. How do you get your head around that?

We drove back to the neighborhood on Tuesday, wood still burning and the air still thick with smoke. I remember parking at the edge of where the fire had been stopped on Bock Road. Looking out across the railroad tracks up towards the hills of Fountaingrove, there was nothing except chimneys and charred trees.

We walked to his home, knowing it was gone, seeing other neighbors standing in their driveways just staring or picking up fragments of anything that was left, which was mostly nothing. I still see vividly what was left of his kitchen. The kitchen that had taken all summer to work on. The two metal stools at the island, fallen over in perfect unison and intact. The stove that we had only made one hot meal on since it had been installed, exploded across what had been the kitchen. It was a ghostly image of what had been there, except now it was now bent and bruised looking.

Since then we have seen the rawest of human compassion. The contributions and support have been abundant. And most things are now measured by whether it happened before or after the fire. Today concrete is getting poured for what will be the foundation of Kevin's new home. There is a bitter sweetness to all of it. Time has helped lessen the shock. Grateful for the exhaustive efforts of the emergency workers and the community. #sonomastrong

Cary Rich

We lived on Old Redwood HWY near River Road/Mark West Springs Road.

On the evening of Sunday, October 8th, 2017, as common practice, I went upstairs at approximately 9:30 p.m. to go to bed. Upon reaching the top of the stairs I noticed a very strong smell of smoke. I called down to my husband and told him that there was a lot of smoke coming through the windows.

He went outside to look for any signs of a fire. I proceeded to look up Fire/Sheriff and Police Websites, access our local newspaper and emergency agencies to find out if there was a fire and how far away it was from us. There was absolutely nothing!

Since I was unable to find anything, and my husband didn't 'see' anything we both figured there was a fire somewhere and that due to the velocity of the winds that night that that was why we were smelling smoke.

My husband stayed up until about 11:30 p.m. and waited and watched for any information about a fire nearby. Nothing! So, he came to bed.

At approximately 12:50 a.m. Monday, October 9, 2017, one hour and twenty minutes after my husband went to bed, he immediately jumped up out of the bed as if a super-natural forced grabbed him by the collar and stood him up on his feet. He very calmly, but eerily and firmly said, "Honey, get up!" "Get up now and get to the car!"

His voice was so firm I knew something was wrong but there was no time for me to question him. I did as he said.

As I was getting up and trying to wake from my groggy state of sleeping my husband proceeded to wake up our 13-year-old son.

As I left our bedroom, our son followed directly behind me with my husband behind him.

We exited out our back door in our pajamas and with nothing else but our car keys. As we exited I saw my purse sitting on a stool next to the kitchen counter, so I grabbed it.

(Approximately three days before the fire I had transferred all of our credit cards and check books to my purse something I never do).

At 1:05 a.m. on Monday, October 9th, 2017, the three of us got into the car. I was driving. As I pulled out of our driveway I looked North toward the intersection of Mark West Springs Road and Old Redwood Hwy. I could see a lot of lights. I made a quick decision to head South on Old Redwood Hwy in hopes of avoiding traffic. I'm glad I did!

As I was driving down the road my husband was trying to contact our adult children on his cell phone. Our 20-year-old daughter and her husband, newly-weds of 1 year, lived in the same neighborhood but we couldn't get through.

However, as fate would have it, the two of them drove up alongside of us as we headed south down Old Redwood HWY. Thankfully, we were together and headed toward our other daughter's home just South of Coffey Park.

We arrived at approximately 1:30 a.m., about twenty-five minutes' after fleeing our home.

As we arrived we were able to make contact by cell phone and our daughter's husband opened their front door and proceed to get air mattresses out for us to sleep on.

We just knew everything was going to be ok. We would get some sleep and head back home in the morning. However, just as we were getting ready to get in bed our daughter received a Nixle report that the fire had jumped the freeway and that Coffey Park was on Fire.

Because we were so close to Coffey Park we decided to leave and began trying to contact friends and family.

We drove a little further south (North Dutton) to our other daughter's home to warn them. There was a little time for them to get gas and then we headed South. We avoided the freeway and took back roads until we reached Petaluma Hill Road and we made our way to our niece's home at the border of Rohnert Park.

When we arrived at our niece's home, we could see a bright orange sky rising above Crane Canyon. It appeared to be moving pretty quickly so we decided to continue driving south. We continued on Petaluma Hill Road until we reached

Rohnert Park Expressway and then got on the freeway at that point and continued driving.

There was 12 of us in three cars following each other toward San Rafael. We pulled into a motel seeking refuge but there were no vacancies. By now it was about 3:30 a.m.

One of our daughters contacted her boss and told him what was going on. He was able to set us up in an Extended Stay type of temporary housing. He paid for the 12 of us to stay for 2 weeks.

During that first morning at approximately 11a.m. we found out that we had, in fact, lost our home. Having been self-employed as home child care providers for the 27 years, we also lost our business.

The initial news of finding out about our total loss was complete shock and a feeling of devastation. We were now walking through the day as if in a fog.

With no underwear or bra and only dressed in my pajamas I was tasked with shopping for some bare necessities for our family.

Exactly 2 weeks after the fires ravaged through our community evacuation had lifted me, my husband our thirteen-year-old son, our youngest daughter and her husband all moved in to a 2 bedroom, 1 ½ bath leased by one of our daughters, her husband and their almost 2-year-old daughter.

Still weary of the devastation we had to work quickly to figure out a source of income and where to live.

We were one of the lucky ones. We had just purchased an RV in 2016, although not knowing how to use it yet, we were literally baptized by fire. A lovely family offered their property and allowed us to move our RV onto their property.

My husband's brand-new tow vehicle burned in the fire, so we had to have a friend move us. Unfortunately, his mother and all of his siblings also lost their homes and were trying to get their RV's to other locations. We were added to the list. One week later, approximately three weeks after the fires we were able to have our RV transported from storage to where we would, now, call home.

It took an additional week to get our utilities hooked-up, our water and dumping service set-up and we officially moved into our RV full-time the Friday before Halloween.

While managing these new details we were still focused on working with Licensing to figure out a way to operate our day care. Thankfully, they allowed us to operate our day care in the home of our daughter, also a licensed day care provider, with a six-month waiver.

We were able to officially re-open our day care as an infant center operating out of facilities offered to us by a local church. We officially opened April 2, 2018.

As a way of honoring our community we chose a name that would represent all of our strength and perseverance. We are called Santa Rosa Rise and Shine Child Care Center.

The trials are not over and there is a lot of work still to be done, but we are blessed as we continue to look toward the future.

Brittany Ann

June 4 · Santa Rosa, CA

My parents lost their home in the Tubbs fire. They lived in Coffey Park on Crestview Drive.

 My mom and sister had planned back in March a surprise 50th birthday trip for my Dad to Hawaii, he had never been before. So, the count down from March to October began. They arrived in Hawaii October 6th. Their first day (or first few hours) were packed full of fun and memories.

My Fiancé, my daughter and I had stayed behind in Santa Rosa at our home. We always sleep with our bedroom window open upstairs. At midnight I woke my fiancé up and asked him to close the window because my eyes were burning, I just figured it was our neighbors next door having their nightly bonfires outback.

 I fell asleep again and was woken by my fiancé handing me the phone at 3:26am telling me it was my Dad and he had to talk to me. I was half asleep when I got onto the phone. His first words were "I need to tell you something and I need you to stay calm." The first thing that ran through my mind was there was an accident in Hawaii and I wasn't sure if it was my mom or my sister that was hurt. He then began to tell me that our neighbor called him as he is running for his life out of neighborhood to let him know that our street is on fire.

He then asked me if was safe (we lived at the time 7 minutes from my parents' house) I started freaking out telling my Dad I had to get off the phone and go get what I can save. (Little did I know our house had already been burned to nothing 30 minutes ago) my Dad on the phone was begging me to stay away from Crestview Drive.

He then begged me to start packing whatever I need and to get my fiancé and my 2-year-old packed in the car and head South. He was terrified that we were going to become grid locked with everyone trying to escape and wanted us away from Santa Rosa and safe. We ended up driving to Bloomfield to my fiancé's best friend's house where we stayed through the night.

The next morning, I had friends sending me pictures of my parents' house. It was all gone. I had to see for myself. So, I left my fiancé and daughter safe at our friend's house and I drove over.

As soon as I started driving by Schafer elementary, some emotion I've never in my life felt hit me. Everything was gone. I remember driving down Coffey Lane right at San Miguel and there being downed power lines. Fear didn't even keep me from driving past it. I was so numb.

I remember driving up to my parents' house and having to make the phone call to confirm to them that their house, street and neighborhood was gone. I stayed long enough to take pictures to send them because the gas and water lines were so loud and leaking. Two days later, (my parents still in Hawaii) called me. It was my Dad calling to let me know that our cat "B" was found near our home that burnt and was brought in. He stayed at RP VCA for a few days before being transferred to UC Davis to treat his burns. He's back with my parents at their new home.

Susan Ault

I was born in Shasta County in 1951 I lived most of my life in what we up here call "the Real Northern California"

I felt anger and frustration as I watched this inferno take over the areas I use to live in rode my horse in, camped, hunted and fished in.

My dad was a Lumber man starting with logging del Monte properties in 1939 and as he moved from outdoors to inside as shipping foreman for Kimberly Clark, I listened. He was mad then about forest mismanagement and since the "old growth and spotted owl movements of the 70's and 80's" it's only gotten worse.

Loggers can't do what they once did: Clean the forest floors, build roads, cut old, dead or diseased trees.

As I watched this fire rage over the county I love, I found myself burning with the same intensity toward the poor management of our local forest that allowed this fire to cause such utter devastation.

We, as a society who live in this beautiful area, need to let our voices be heard

THIS IS NOT climate change. We haven't had 120-degree days like when I grew up here

THIS has everything to do with politicians pushing an agenda and not caring for the people they are sworn to serve.

Kelly Eash

Well I am interested in reading it. There was never a time in my life where I cared to know the area history, until I moved to Sonoma County in 2003 when beginning a new job and new life after divorce. Reading the stories of fellow county residents matters to me as well.

What happened was real. Although in Forestville, and not directly affected by flame, the quality of air we breathed was compromised. Opportunist jumped up and onto the band wagon wrapping themselves in blankets of sympathy being handed out.

True victims were less vocal, I believe. Some humble even, kept moving forward, no matter the difficulty. Others may be suffering still, emotionally, physically, financially. But we are still here. My friends.

Tina Schlaile

Like most Californians, I was horrified at the events which struck Santa Rosa, California the night of October 8, 2017. Whole neighborhoods decimated, homes engulfed and burned to the ground in just a matter of minutes, the same amount of time many had to flee for their lives. In the chaos of that night, few had the presence of mind to grab mementos or precious family heirlooms and these, along with other reminders of their lives, succumbed to the whims of a wildfire hot enough to melt silver and gold.

Three years previously, I had called Santa Rosa home. The worst events I experienced during that time were one small earthquake and a no seat belt ticket. On October 10, I returned to see this city's new reality and was unprepared for what I saw. Home sites were still smoking, so were the shoulders along Highway 101 along with the businesses that used to line the frontage road. People out walking near the burned areas looked shocked and stunned.

The smoke in the air hung heavy and thick, and you could easily look up and stare at the sun. Affected neighborhoods were blocked off, hampered by power outages and nonfunctioning traffic lights. I returned home to Fairfield in a state of disbelief, only to see the enormous cloud of smoke billowing from the Atlas Fire less than six miles away.

For the next month and a half, I watched the local news, sickened at early reports of over 400 people missing and worried that number seemed too small. I tried to think of ideas of how best to help this community, but every potential plan was already in use or surpassed my qualifications for the job. By pure chance, I happened to catch TV coverage of a volunteer group sifting through a fire victim's home. I could not sign up fast enough.

My first assignment was located in the Stone Creek subdivision off Fountain Grove Drive. I was the first volunteer to arrive that day and slowly drove past what was left of destroyed homes, checking address numbers printed on bright green metal sign posts placed in each front yard. Aside from an occasional surviving mailbox, this was the only way to identify a residence. Finding the right site, I pulled over and parked, my attention now drawn to a lone woman standing at the foot of the driveway.

Damn. Although my car sat less than 30 feet away, this woman never turned her head. There was a cleanup crew or two nearby, running large excavators, but they were far enough away where the noise wasn't intrusive. I took one last glance in my rearview mirror, hoping to see another volunteer arriving but saw no one. I got out and quietly walked up to the woman.

"Hi," I said sheepishly, "My name is Tina and I'm one of the sifting volunteers. Are you the home owner?" Her sad expression and a slight nod gave me my answer.

I don't remember if I told her anything like "sorry for your loss" but the pile of rubble and ashes lying at the other end of her driveway were hard to ignore. A few objects in the debris looked familiar; a washer and dryer, a furnace or fridge but so much more was unidentifiable—all shapes and sizes of metal parts, many damaged and twisted into grotesque figurines. Globs of melted glass, wires, tile, broken dishware, pipes and nails were also present, lying scattered within a dusty layer of ash about five inches thick...the only evidence left of what used to be a 1500 square foot house. Two months later I'd be able to identify everything from a phone battery to a drawer slide, but for now the scene before me defied explanation or definition.

"Are you here by yourself or is anyone else coming?" the homeowner asked, breaking my concentration.

"No, there will be more people," I answered, not able to give an exact number.

"How many other homes have you sifted?"

Damn, again.

Electing to be truthful, I admitted, "This is my first, but I've got a good eye for detail...what items are you looking for?"

As time went on, conversations with fire victims became easier, but it was never easy to know what best to say. Many didn't seem to mind retelling their "fire stories." A few received phone calls from relatives, friends or neighbors; others either smelled smoke or suddenly realized their backyard was on fire. None of the victims I spoke to ever got a reverse 911 call or had a first responder tell them to evacuate.

One couple I helped lived at the end of a long driveway near Glen Ellen; their closest neighbor about 200 yards away. The narrow lane between the two homes hugs the side of a hill and winds around a steep gully. The surrounding vegetation is composed of pine trees, scrub oak, Manzanita and thick bush. The couple's home was rather unique, a one-story adobe-like building with nearly 2-foot-thick earthen walls and a flat, asphalt and pebble-coated roof which now composed the top layer of flooring. It looked odd, at least from a sifter's point of view, as there was hardly any visible ash. Digging through this tar-like substance wasn't easy, but eventually I spotted a palm-sized clay frog nearly hidden in the debris, and handed it to the husband standing nearby, expecting nothing more than a kind acknowledgement for finding an intact, but unremarkable, knick-knack.

"Oh my God, I can't believe you found that!"

Despite the joy of hearing that sentence numerous times, I had rarely seen a man so close to tears over a little figurine. His explanation was rather remarkable. He had once saved members of a poor family in Mexico, and the frog was one of their few personal possessions. They gave it to him as gratitude for his heroism. I would have never imagined that little frog's significance.

The rest of this couple's fire story was just as remarkable. Both were home that night, the wife recuperating in bed after knee surgery and the husband watching TV in the living room. The patio door leading to the back yard was behind him, and he soon noticed an odd light reflection on the TV screen. He turned around to investigate and was horrified to see flames lighting up his backyard. He dashed to the bedroom and prepared to get his wife out to the car. Owning two cats, they grabbed the pet carriers, but the felines only ran and hid under the bed. Unable to capture either one and with only seconds to spare, the couple fled their burning home and drove down the hill towards the main road. The only light illuminating their escape route were the flames burning along the shoulder. I drove that road in the daytime and only comfortably at a slow speed.

One day, we had another home to sift over in Mark West Estates. Again, I was there before others and met one of the homeowners, an elderly man, waiting in the front yard. As was normal by that time, I had him point out the areas he wanted searched, along with a description of the missing items. He mentioned wanting to locate a shotgun stored in a coat closet near the front door and that his wife's jewelry lay somewhere inside a small addition added to the house a few years ago. Another area of interest lay towards the rear of the house, so we started to walk around the perimeter. I happened to glance down and noticed what looked like the remains of a revolver lying in the ash. I retrieved the gun and held it up for the homeowner. The shocked look on his face threw me.

"I can't believe you just found that, lying right there!"

After he repeated what he'd said, the gentleman took the revolver and cradled it with care in his hands. We eventually found what was left of the shotgun, along with a few charred pieces of the wife's jewelry. I don't recall the significance of that revolver, but often times it wasn't unusual for fire victims to forget about certain belongings.

This happened while we were sifting through a couple's home in Coffey Park. Both were women and one was several months pregnant. They had just purchased the house in September and still had much of their stuff packed in boxes inside the garage. The women had previously searched the site and found some keepsakes, but deciding to leave a few items there overnight, returned the next day to find the most valuable things gone. Aside from some jewelry, one owner was anxious to find a dog tag that belonged to former pet, along with the animal's ashes inside a container. Both items, she said, were left on top of the refrigerator.

Initially, my hopes soared. The fridge was still standing upright, in the middle of the house, although looking like the roof had landed on top of it. Still, to have such a small search area was a sifter's dream. Nearly an hour and a half later, after thoroughly searching a radius of about five feet around the appliance I had found neither item. This wasn't a surprise. The high winds that accompanied the October fires pushed weakened structures over sideways, instead of allowing them to collapse internally. Once airflow entered the home, the items on top of the fridge could've landed anywhere. Tired and frustrated, I asked a fellow sifter if she wanted to trade places, as oftentimes a fresh set of eyes can help tremendously. She agreed and within about ten minutes, proudly held up a blackened aluminum dog tag! For the next hour we continued working, waiting with gleeful anticipation for the return of the homeowner from a doctor's appointment. When shown the tag, she immediately burst into tears. It did not belong to the dog originally thought, but to a second one which had also died. As far as I know, the other tag and ash container were never found, but for one pet owner, that loss was lessened by the return of something equally as important.

One pleasant afternoon, our sifting group was up in Fountain Grove, planning to sift what was once a two-story house. The renter who use to live there, was at work but available for phone calls. Essentially, she only wanted a small collection of jewelry left in a box inside her bedroom closet on the second floor. We narrowed down the most likely area and started to dig. An hour and a half later, we'd sifted through an area about 10 feet square, but only found a few metal drawer slides. I called the renter with a new set of questions and feeling satisfied returned to work.

Another hour and a half passed before we had cleared an area twice as large but still nothing tangible to show for our efforts. Even though it was time for us to pack up and leave, we decided to "give it another 15 minutes." This phrase, which we'd muttered before, held several meanings. The first, as a good luck token—we'd found numerous rings and other valuables in the last 5 or 10 minutes of a shift, despite looking previously for hours. Secondly, as a plea or prayer, to a higher power than ourselves, to direct our eyes and hands to an item's location that only God knew where. And lastly, as a group affirmation that none of us were ready to give up searching.

Unfortunately, a half hour later, we were still empty-handed and the setting sun dwindling our light source. I grabbed a couple of shovels and walked out to the street to place the tools inside of our truck. Upon returning, I walked past what had used to be the front entrance and the kitchen area to my left. I happened to glance down... and saw a ring. I stood there, half mad, half elated, and growled, "Don't tell me..." The others overheard and with hopeful faces, rushed over. In a matter of minutes, we were on hands and knees, separating bits of jewelry from broken dishes in the fading light of dusk. The distance between where we were in the kitchen to where the bedroom and closet had been, was nearly 20 feet. Because we had stayed longer than usual, the jewelry's owner was able to come by after she got off work. We learned that while the bedroom indeed was on the upper level, the kitchen area had no floor above it.

Several times, by some unexplainable fluke, jewelry would end up on top of everything else. I never postulated an explanation, but as the weeks went by, it became rather pointless as the phenomenon insisted on remaining a mystery. I realize that some items, no matter how miraculous their discovery, were just meant to be found. Other items, despite turning the home upside down and sifting its entire contents, would remain forever lost. Yet, mystery or not, occasionally our efforts proved fruitless, despite knowing exactly where to look.

One sad example happened near the Rincon Ridge subdivision in Fountain Grove. A young family with three kids lost their home and the wife had left some valuables on the fireplace mantle in the upstairs bedroom. Initially, she directed us to one side of the house to look, but after starting to bust through a fallen section of stucco wall, she unexpectedly announced the bedroom was in a totally different area. The trauma of that October night, along (no doubt) with looking at the destroyed remnants of her home, affected her ability to remember the simple layout of the house. Even though we had several workers that day, and easily located what remained of the fireplace, we couldn't find anything salvageable for this family except an unbroken plate or two of common, nondescript dishware.

Unsuccessful discoveries like this home, always hit me hard. While the joy of locating just one special trinket or ceramic piece was a big victory, the heartbreak of not finding a particular family heirloom or something recognizable from a child's bedroom tended to erase any satisfaction from a previous discovery. And the range of items either wanted or not from home owners varied as much as the people themselves. Some wanted practically everything, weather broken or not; others only items which escaped any sign of damage. I believe a determining factor in their decisions was whether they had some place to store their treasures as many stayed in hotel rooms for months after the fires. Another big disappointment was when FEMA began beating us to home sites. A homeowner would call on Monday and schedule a time for Wednesday and then cancel the next day because they'd gotten their 48-hour notice.

I remember thinking towards the end of our sifting work, about how incredible it was to have been part of a once-in-a-lifetime event. Standing in the middle of more destroyed homes in Redding, California this past August, has only made me think of how soon I'll be compelled to go to another community devastated by a wildfire. Honestly, I hope I won't have to...I've seen enough anguish and hurt. Seeing a fire victim's attitude change from despair to elation because you found a precious item is always fulfilling, but it doesn't replace the feeling from losing everything you own. I asked a homeowner recently, if recovery of a few cherished mementos helped them with closure. She answered that each item helped bring another layer of a former time back into her life, of a past birthday, holiday or heirloom from a relative now gone. But, she added sadly, "going through something like this totally shatters your life."

Tiff Bell

I wanted to contribute my story for your book, if you are still wanting stories...

It was about 11pm on October 8th, 2017 when the electricity went out. I remember clearly as I was sitting on my couch, almost done crocheting the blanket for the surrogate baby I was carrying. I was 37 weeks pregnant for a couple in San Francisco. I wanted to stay up and finish the blanket, since delivery was soon for the baby. But since the electricity went out, I figured it was time to try & get some sleep.

I laid in bed, unable to sleep, as the wind was so strong and loud... I remember staring out my window, watching the trees bend and sway, worried some of them would fall.

It was about midnight when my mother came down from upstairs to check on me. She had seen reports of the fire on the other side of the hill and wanted to make sure I was aware as well. We both were worried, but I'm sure like most, we figured the fire would be contained soon and I tried to rest. The power had come back on for a few minutes, but it didn't last long, and it was out again.

It was about 1:20 am when I had finally fallen asleep. I was so thankful, as being so far along in pregnancy, sleep doesn't come easy, and it doesn't last long once it does...

That's when my brother woke me up at about 1:30am, my first thought was how upset I was that he woke me because I had JUST fallen asleep... But then he started telling me that we had to leave. It took a couple minutes to register what he was trying to tell me... And I admittedly didn't really believe him, as if it was just some kind of joke.

But, I got out of bed, walked out into the house, and everyone was awake: my mother, my step-dad, my brother, sister-in-law, my niece who had just turned 1 years old.... (Thankfully, my 8-year-old son was with his dad that night.) I remember my brother getting as much into his car as he could fit, asking if I had extra room in mine. I remember stepping outside the garage and seeing all the ash fall around me, thinking it looked like snow. It all felt surreal, and as if some of it was happening in slow motion... I had gone back into the house and my mother said that we only have one cat carrier, and that I should use it for my cat. I replied that her cat was much more skittish than mine, and I can put a harness on my cat and use a small carryon bag if needed.

The chaos in the house made it impossible to think of what I needed to do, what I needed to grab, what I should take with...

I could only think to ask everyone if they got everything they needed... Their electronics, power cords, clothing...

As I started to load up my car, I was feeling thankful that I had just started to pack my hospital bag that night, so I had my to-go toiletries and laboring clothes. I had also pre-packed my backpack the night before for studying at the coffee shop the next morning, so it had my laptop, my Animal Behavior College study guide book #2, as well as a workout outfit for later. I stuffed in a couple more pairs of workout clothes (which were the only things fitting me at the time). I grabbed a blanket and my pregnancy pillow since I didn't know if where we were going would have those things.

Then I stood in my living room... and slowly turned around, looking at everything in it... all the paintings I had done over the years, my souvenirs from my trip to Europe, all the things I had bought over the years with the hope of them someday going with me when I bought my very own house... I stared at these things, telling myself that that's all they are, "things" ...

My brother said we could all go and spend the night at his wife's dad's condo across town (her dad has passed away a couple months earlier unexpectedly). There wasn't much in his condo as they had been getting it ready to sell. But it was somewhere to go, somewhere 'safe'.

My brother & his family were the first to depart. I didn't want to go – I still thought it was all going to stop. I didn't think the fire would reach our house. Firefighters have always taken care of everything in time... And the fire still felt far away, even though it wasn't... I remember telling myself this only happens on the news and in movies. It will all be here in the morning, and I can come back tomorrow...

I packed up my cat and did the best I could to keep him calm for the drive. Driving away from the house left me feeling awful. Driving through all the ash falling, the trees still bending, now branches are in the road.

We left at about 1:45am. It was terrifying driving with everyone else evacuating. I could hear policemen on loud speakers driving through the area telling everyone to evacuate. Everyone was driving recklessly, and it felt so unsafe to be driving.

When we got to my sister-in-law's dad's condo, we tried to get settled and catch some sleep... My parents had a bed downstairs, my brother & his family on a pull-out couch upstairs with me in a recliner near them... But I didn't get any sleep at all... I had a coworker call me at about 5am checking on me to see if I was safe. I listened to the police radio all night, waiting to hear that they had it under control – but I never got to hear that...

My son called be about 6am, terrified. He was so worried about me, about the family. All I wanted to do was hug him and tell him it would all be ok. That we are all fine, and everything will be just fine. But I also promised myself that I would never lie to him. My son was dropped off with me an hour or so later and I gave him the BIGGEST hug ever!

I wish my story stopped there, but it doesn't.

We lost everything we had. All the schoolwork my son had done over the years, all his toys; his feeling of safety.

We wanted to stay together, and I needed to be near a Sutter Hospital for my surrogacy. We decided to drive to the Sacramento area where we wouldn't have to worry about being evacuated again and to be away from the smoke and ash.

Luckily, I had a friend in that area as well and she took me out shopping to get some necessities: clothes, toiletries, food... She took me to Target to get these things, and when we were almost done shopping, the lights went out at the store and my son became terrified, worried that the fire had followed us.

When we got back to the hotel, my son was in our room on the third floor with the family, when my friend & I went down to the first floor to wash the clothes we bought at the second-hand store. That's when it got worse. The fire alarms went off at the Hotel. I lost it, which is not normal for me. I've always been someone to stay calm during emergencies, but all I could think was that my son was up in our room, possibly alone, terrified.

I ran up the stairs to get to him, and he was so distraught. It took me probably hours to fully calm myself down.

The Thursday after the fires, we relocated to an Air BnB in Sebastopol. This was the very worst part of all of it. Mentally, I can acknowledge my house burning down, and all my belongings, all my son's belongings, my family's things, my grandmothers things (including her ashes), but the absolute worst part of all of this, happened now. The fires caused my beloved cat to get too sick. He had a rough year, which included a surgery to help with his bladder stones. But stress triggers his stones to form, and moving from place to place was just too hard on him, and he was now consistently in so much pain that I couldn't keep him around because I needed him... I am still so heartbroken by this, he was a huge part of my family. I got him as a bottle-fed kitten, before my son was even born. He was only 9 years old and my son loved him as much as I did. This still hurts to even think about.

We spent 10 days at the place in Sebastopol & then moved to a Hotel in Healdsburg. During this stay was the second hardest thing to deal with. My brother & his family decided to move to Oregon. They had nothing left in Santa Rosa to stay for, nothing to their names, and couldn't afford to stay since, like me, they did not have renter's insurance. Again, my son was heartbroken. His cousin was moving away, and they were as close as siblings... More than dealing with my own grief, dealing with trying to help my son through all of this has been so hard. He's always been a sensitive kid, and he has struggled with PTSD since the fires, as have I.

After 10 days in Healdsburg, on November 1st, I delivered a surrogate baby for the couple in San Francisco (they had a healthy baby girl!). I spent a couple days in the hospital to recover, then moved into my great aunt's mobile home in a senior park (she had been moved into a care facility when the fires happened, as she had Alzheimer's and dementia). I spent the next couple nights sleeping on a floor because we had no furniture yet. I remember the first night there, because I was alone, and struggled to feel safe enough to fall asleep. That was when I had my first PTSD Nightmare. I remember waking up in a panic, thinking someone was yelling at me to get out...

I tried to go back to work after my maternity leave but was having a really difficult time trying to contain my PTSD and anxiety. I still struggle with this, and I feel like I'm failing at recovering from everything that has happened. I have been dealing with mood swings and emotional distress for the last several months, which has caused my doctor to put me on medical leave. I want so badly to be strong for my son, but every day is a challenge.

I try so hard to be 'normal' again but find it difficult to have 'things'. I want my son to have his childhood, but how do I do that when I struggle to buy a board game, or a new toy, or some trinket...

I want to say that I've reached the end of my story, but I'm not sure if this type of story every really ends... I've made in into a more permanent house with my parents and my son, but it's not Home... I'm not sure when anything will feel like home again...

Daniel Gonnella

On the night of Oct 8th, Occidental Fire Dept and Occidental Cal Fire extinguished part of the Tubbs Fire that was spreading in a field next to Brush Creek Nursery School in Santa Rosa. By their actions that night, the crews saved the school from burning.

To our surprise, we received the most thoughtful thank you from the faculty, students and families of Brush Creek Nursery School. They arranged for pizza and dessert from the Union Hotel be delivered to our station tonight. While eating we all enjoyed passing around all the thank you notes and drawings from the students. We will frame some and put all the others in albums for people to enjoy.

On behalf of the men and women of Occidental Fire Dept and Occidental Cal Fire, Thank you Brush Creek Nursery School

I've heard many horrific stories both personally and from friends on Facebook. These stories can't not change you. Here is but one excerpt from a post:

"escorted by the National Guard into one of the devastated neighborhoods yesterday. I stared in silence and disbelief at what I saw. Everything was destroyed, as far as the eye could see.

"Chimneys stood like tombstones for each of the homesites. The air was filled with toxic smoke. I couldn't bear to take pictures, it felt wrong, disrespectful even.

"I snapped only one - of the melted metal coming from a car. Like candle wax it flowed down the driveway. I later learned it was the engine block, which begins to melt at 1200 degrees Fahrenheit.

"The average house fire hits 1100 degrees. There was nothing average about this firestorm.

"We spent the day in line at FEMA (which had an amazing set up, allowing people to not only apply for help - but to go from line to line replacing birth certificates, social security cards, licenses, passports). We went shopping for more household items, thankfully Ryan and his family have found a temporary home. Tears were frequent, of gratitude."

10-9

Santa Rosa is under siege by wildfire. Need divine intervention. Many, many homes and businesses lost...too many to comprehend. Still raging. Please pray for our citizenry.

Probably 1000 homes gone. Unbelievable.

10-10

SRPD: Residents in the Annadel Heights area, bordered north by Parktrail Drive and west by Summerfield Road, need to evacuate immediately.

Being attacked from both North and South. Annadel, Oakmont, and Wikiup. Heaven help us.

10-12

Update: 15 fire-related deaths expected to go higher, 2800 houses lost within the city of Santa Rosa (doesn't include unincorporated Larkfield and Wikiup...probably another 800 or more homes lost), 400 people still missing.

Mission restaurant (Rincon Valley) is still closed because of no electricity. Electric and natural gas is spotty in the Rincon Valley area. College Ave restaurant still closed because of no natural gas.

10-14

(Español abajo)

The following eastern Santa Rosa locations are now under Mandatory Evacuation:

Hwy 12 between Adobe Canyon Rd in Kenwood and Calistoga Rd in Santa Rosa. This includes both sides of Hwy 12 and any/all side roads in between.

Everybody needs to evacuate westbound on Hwy 12 to Santa Rosa immediately.

Please evacuate area immediately. Check Sheriff's Office Facebook or Sonoma County EOC Hotline 707-565-3856.

For anybody who needs alternate transportation, there are buses staged at Safeway at Hwy 12 / Calistoga Rd

Las siguientes ubicaciones al este de Santa Rosa están sujetas a Evacuación Obligatoria:

Carreter 12 entre Adobe Canyon Rd en Kenwood y Calistoga Rd en Santa Rosa. Esto incluye ambos lados de la carretera 12 y cualquiera/todos los caminos laterales entre estas calles.

Todas las personas deben de evacuar inmediatamente en dirección al oeste de la carretera 12 hacia Santa Rosa.

Por favor evacuen el área inmediatamente. Cheque la página de Facebook de la Oficina del Alguacil o la línea de emergencia del EOC del Condado de Sonoma en el 707-565-3856

Cualquier persona que necesita transporte alterno, hay camiones estacionados en el Safeway que está en la carretera 12 y el Calistoga Rd

I noticed myself not hitting the "Like" button anymore, it's either the "Love" button or the "Tears" button. 😢

I just want to say to all my friends out of the area, whatever you see on the news, it's worse than that.

10-15

Here's more info about what fire life is like:

Reality right now.

We walk around in masks, and know what N95 means

We regularly ask if you "saw flames or just smoke"

We gather in parking lots to watch our hillside, discuss "back fire," and argue over white vs black smoke

We end conversations with strangers with "Be Safe"

We have stayed off the roads when possible, and feel anxious the further away and the longer away from home we get

We get ash on ourselves just being outside a minute

We hear helicopters and sirens REGULARLY

We see emergency and military vehicles constantly, and coming from all over the Bay Area

We haven't hiked, walked at the lake, run, or picnicked in DAYS - daily activities and stress reliefs for many of us

We have had our stuff packed and been on alert for days in a row

We spend the night at different places

We have limited clothes at times

We live minute to minute, and thus can't plan easily

We are sleep deprived, exercise deprived, OUTSIDE deprived

We are stressed, shell shocked, relieved, grateful, guilty (why is my home spared?), worried, unknowing if home is gone

We have been stripped of our routine, belongings, and control

We listen to the radio

We argue a LOT with loved ones about evacuating or not

We don't quite know what to do

We are in coping / helping mode and haven't quite wrapped our mind around this

We're even more SENTIMENTAL and NOSTALGIC than usual

In Sonoma County you'll see thick smoke, burned hills and neighborhoods, intersections without lights (stop at these), barricades ready to be put up, middle lanes blocked for emergency vehicles, closed stores, distracted and overwhelmed customer service people - BE NICE, emptier streets, closed stores, and emergency vehicles from ALL OVER. You'll see "THANK YOU" signs EVERYWHERE for our first responders and emergency personnel. You'll see our typical SoCo generosity.

Wear a mask if you can. Drive cautiously and stop at intersections even if lights are out. Don't drive in the left lane - or at least always check the rearview mirror for emergency vehicles coming behind you. If you see a horse trailer, give it some room. They aren't going on a trail ride, they are evacuating livestock. Check where there are road closures and know that info is impossible to be completely up to the minute accurate. Be patient.

Sonoma County is pretty beat up right now, but she's still her awesome self.

#repost

#somomastrong

#norcalstrong

(Copied and pasted)

8:30 a.m. Mission Boulevard and Highway 12: the first morning in 6 with no rising smoke or flames on the ridgeline. There is a slight smoky haze.

I might add, I also saw a 6-engine strike team leaving the fire area. I'm not sure if they were going home, or to the staging area for a new assignment. At least 2 of the trucks were from Reno...Thank you.

It's been one week since the fires started, so many people lost everything and it's still not over. This really makes you take a long minute to realize what's important and what's not. To see everyone come together is so amazing and I'm so blessed to have so many loved ones! I'm so sorry to all that were affected by this tragedy! I hope it will end and we will come together and build our beautiful county again! Union hotel is open! So, if you need a little get away come on in! It's nice to at least be together when at this time feels like we have nothing. Love you all and hope to see you! Have a blessed Sunday! ♡ 🙏🏻🙇 #sonomastrong

10-16

Monday morning 8:30, day 8: Three strike teams just went by heading east towards the fire. Smoke is rising but it is behind the Ridgeline from my vantage point at Mission Boulevard and Highway 12. A lone fire truck from Bullhead City Arizona heading west.

Business was as close to normal as it could be last night, however I would say we were about 95% credit cards as opposed to the 75% norm.

#winecountrystrong

#santarosastrong

Comment on my earlier post.

"Yes, I got this from my neighbor this morning.

"OK here's an update, just talked with Jeremy who is with Marin County fire and lives just above us on Vista Ridge. The fire did actually jump their initial line, but there are 50 bulldozers 39 helicopters and 27 fixed wing aircraft that are assigned to the area. They are cutting another Fire line from Skyhawk past Yerba Buena and going to continue it up to the ridge all the way to Calistoga Road. They do not believe that there is any imminent threat to Skyhawk or Rincon Valley today.

"But then they lifted he evac notices for Kenwood and glen Ellen. Just not Rincon valley

25 firemen from Los Angeles walked in for dinner just now. They received a standing ovation walking through the dining room. They take care of us, we took care of their bill. Thank you, Los Angeles Fire!

#payitforward

#santarosastrong

#winecountrystrong

10-17

Tuesday 8:00 a.m., day 9: These pictures were taken at Mission Boulevard and Highway 12. Much less smoke this morning. I just saw a strike team from San Francisco heading east into the fire zone, and a strike team from Ventura County heading west. I finally get the sense this may be coming to an end.

If you saw my post from last night, I should have added the City of Angels grew a little bit in my heart. Thank you, Los Angeles and countless other communities, that I've seen, both police and fire, from all over the western United States.

10-18

"We spent the day in line at FEMA (which had an amazing set up, allowing people to not only apply for help - but to go from line to line replacing birth certificates, social security cards, licenses, passports). We went shopping for more household items, thankfully Ryan and his family have found a temporary home. Tears were frequent, of gratitude."

Derek Shaffer

May 31 at 3:48pm

Have been seeing a lot of people not able to find a home lately on the posts and wanted to give some

outside perspective. I couldn't find anywhere to live either. After a couple frustrating/depressing

months I decided to pack up the very few things I had anymore and drove to Nevada. I am now in a 1-

bedroom place with utilities paid for 875/month. The same kind of situation in SR would be around 1900

a month which is ridiculous. I, no doubt, would love to still be in my community, but it's almost

impossible to still be there until things rebuild.

So, for all the people struggling to find somewhere to live, I would recommend looking elsewhere for the

time being. I signed a 6-month lease to see how things are back in SR at that time and maybe I'll be able to afford to come back. But, unless you have a high-profile job, the price to live there now is just flat out

unfair and not even a life. It's just paying to barely survive and after the fire, we, as fire victims, need to have the opportunity to experience things that bring us joy. To try and get over the pain of losing

everything and being in SR now doesn't really give those chances financially.

 Which is why I recommend looking at the Sacramento area or even move out of state like myself. I

moved to the greater Las Vegas area to get back around old friends as I lived here 4 years ago, and it has

helped my mindset and depression being around familiar faces. I didn't want to leave; but I was virtually

forced to. I feel for everyone struggling and hopefully things change soon, and we can all get back to

our community we love.

Kathryn Kubota

Life the day before and days, weeks and months after the Tubbs Fire

October 7, 2017

For us, the weekend of the fire had already been eventful. Our son, Nolan was visiting from Tucson. Marshall and I had horseback riding lessons early Saturday morning, October 7, 2017. Up to this point it was a usual day. During my lesson, my horse stumbled, and I shifted my weight, which caused her to stumble more and drop her left shoulder. I fell off and went right underneath her hooves. I lost a layer of skin from my left elbow and the inner aspect of the left upper arm took a direct hit with another hoof. To this day I have a hoof print on my arm and a scar on my elbow. I slammed to the ground on my left hip. All this was my own fault because I wasn't using my usual gear. The saddle didn't fit me, and the stirrups were too long. I would have gotten back on, but I was bleeding too much. The last photo taken in our family room was of me smiling, showing off my injuries. The rest of Saturday, Marshall finished putting up the Edison lights we had gotten for the backyard. We had just purchased new patio furniture and were getting ready to have a pool party celebrating the last of the warm weather. Marshall got all the lights up, but I never did get to see all them.

Sunday morning, October 8, 2017, I woke up and couldn't walk. I had injured myself in the fall. I've had multiple kidney stones x12, so I have pain meds. I took enough meds so that I could make it downstairs and to the hospital. There I was checked and scanned and released with just a severe groin strain.

The rest of Sunday was a quiet day for us after we got back from the hospital. Marshall was feeling like he was getting a cold. I was in bed resting. Our security camera recorded Nolan leaving home for the last time. He was heading to the airport, never imagining he wouldn't see his childhood home again. Around 9:30 Sunday night we were watching television and the power went off, and then came right back on. Nothing unusual. About 10 pm we went to sleep.

I awoke to a pounding on the front door. Next, I heard Marshall yelling to get up. I also heard all the battery backup alarms going off. Outside, I heard an announcement over a loud speaker, that we needed to leave right now, that our neighborhood was on fire.

It was all very confusing. Waking up from being sound asleep, to lots of yelling. I put on some shoes and went to get a robe. The first robe I felt was a robe I did care for and was planning on giving way. I tried to grab another. Unfortunately, they all fell to the floor, and I tried a couple of times to grab a different robe. It seemed no matter how I tried to grab another, I kept coming up with the same robe. Oh well, it was just for a while.

The light in our bedroom I realized weeks later was not from the street light, because we had no power. It was from the fire.

This is the record from our home security system.

October 9, 2017

1:40:57 am – The front door was opened

1:41:04 am – The front door was closed

1:41:51 am – The front door was opened

1:41:55 am – The front door was closed

1:42:44 am – The front door was opened

1:45:16 am - The front door was closed

1:52:40 am – The interior garage door was opened

1:52:08 am – The interior garage door was closed

1:52:43 am – The interior garage door was opened

1:53:52 am – The garage door was opened

1:53:59 am – The interior garage door was closed

1:54:01 am – The garage door was closed

When I first stepped outside it was like something out of a nightmare. No movie could ever capture the sights, sounds and feelings. It was hot, my car registered the outside temperature as 82 degrees. It should have been in the mid to lower 50s. The winds were unusually strong, blowing in an obvious counter-clockwise direction. There was debris blowing around us and hitting us. When I looked to my left, it looked like a waterfall, but it wasn't water, there were embers churning down the hillside. The homes on that had once overlooked our neighborhood were gone. The entire hillside was engulfed. Looking forward, toward Mark West it was all lit up by fire. When I looked to my right, I could see the fire coming over the hills. I could see Cardinal Newman was on fire. It looked like the areas around Sutter Hospital were on fire.

Our street looked like a roaring river, but again, it wasn't water, embers were roaring down the street, churning upon themselves. Everything they were touching was starting on fire. Plants, trees, homes, and cars, nothing was immune.

I knew from the moment I stepped outside, I would never see our home of 30+ years again. I'd grown up staying during the summers with my aunt and uncle at Big Hill Lookout in El Dorado County. We had fires regularly, but I had once seen a fire storm. I knew I was seeing a fire storm again. I also knew what that meant. All would be lost. The fire would be too hot and too fast until the weather changed.

We closed our garage door for the last time and got into our Yukon. I started calling neighbors. My neighbor across the street had heard all the noise but had gone back to bed. I told him to put some shoes on and leave, there would soon be no oxygen. I called a neighbor 2 doors away. He was still in his home. I told him he had to leave now, or he would be dying. He picked up the other neighbor and followed us out of the neighborhood.

My next-door neighbor's house was on fire when I left. The neighbor who is catty corner to me luckily had left with their family earlier, because their home was burning. The neighborhood across from us was burning.

As we headed to Mark West Springs Road we called our son Evan, who lived at the corner of Hopper and Coffee. We told him we had no idea what had happened (one thought had been did North Korea finally get fed up. I knew we weren't ground zero, but had San Francisco been hit?). As we were talking to him, he heard a crash outside his bedroom window. He looked outside and said, "a tree just fell on my fence". Then he said, "don't come this way Hoppers on fire". He had to get his family up, put shoes on them, grab their dogs and leave immediately.

As we were leaving our subdivision, it looked like the Luther Burbank Center was burning. Everything was on fire, everything. At Old Redwood Highway there were sheriff deputies trying to help evacuate us. My heart goes out to them. The sounds of their voices will never leave me. They were controlled, but you could hear they were desperate to get us out. They weren't going to leave us, but you could tell they were worried. They stayed and helped us, instead of checking on their own families. They were screaming for us to go, but out of habit we were all doing your turn, my turn.

My next-door neighbor was the Sheriff who used the loudspeaker on his truck to tell us all to leave. He told me after the fire, that our politeness was one of the most frustrating things he had ever experienced. He thought we were going to all die being law-abiding and polite.

When the fire crossed over the freeway we no longer able to go South. They were telling us to take all the lanes North on Old Redwood Highway. Taking over the Southbound lanes as well. Next, we were told to make lanes. There were just too many vehicles, and fire was pushing in on us. When we came to a street we would leave room, thinking that you are not supposed to block streets, in case an emergency vehicle needed to get by. We weren't thinking we were the emergency.

I called one of my brothers, who lives in Washington State. I told him, I didn't know what happened, but that everything was on fire, including cells towers. I wanted him to know Evan and his family and Marshall and I were fine, but not together. Also, I didn't know when I'd be able to get in contact with him again.

Everything is on fire behind us, to the right and left of us. Everything.

When we got up to Airport Blvd the sheriff officers were still directing traffic. The freeway was closed going South, so I went North. I realized that in our immediate area things were not going well and it could get worse. I took the Shiloh exit, crossed the overpass and filled up with gas. Luckily, I always had left my purse in my vehicle locked in the garage or I wouldn't have had a driver's license, credit card or any money. After we filled the car with gas I headed to a friend and neighbors' veterinary clinic on Conde. I was planning on just sitting in the parking lot and getting my thoughts together. When we arrived, our friends were already there. We sat in the clinic for quite a while trying to get in touch with everyone we knew. Our children, who are all grown now, and had long ago abandoned Facebook, once the old people started getting on it. Even they started getting in touch with people through Facebook to make sure their friends' parents were aware of the danger. After it appeared that we had contacted everyone we could, Marshall and I decided to go back out to our vehicle. I parked facing towards home and we could see that the light was brighter, the fire was spreading quickly. I made and received a few calls in those late hours, but mostly listened to the radio.

Evan had barely made it from the corner of Coffee and Hopper, where they had to drive through embers with the children. Their oldest daughter was terrified, the youngest thought it was cool. About the time they were passing Coddingtown their neighbor from across the cul-de-sac sent them a security video feed showing their house catching on fire.

When the sun came up, no one had slept. We said goodbye to our friends and decided to go get some essentials. We always had planned for an earthquake, both in the car and at home. The only thing that was of any value really was the solar radio.

We had heard that Target was sending people from outside the fire area to open the Coddingtown Target. First, we needed to get our medications. I had left wearing a nightgown, robe and shoes. Marshall wore sweatpants, sweatshirt and gardening clogs.

When we got to Target, people there had the same vacant look. People were dressed in everything you could imagine. After ordering our essential meds, we stood in the middle of the isle and had to think about how you start your day. We brush our teeth, it was a starting point. We needed a toothbrush, toothpaste, razor, deodorant, and a comb. We each got a couple pair of underwear and 1 shirt and 1 pair of pants. Everything we owned we could carry in a Target bag.

After we left, we headed to Marshall's office in Santa Rosa. We used the emergency radio to be kept up on what was happening in our community. We could crank it and charge our phones. We contacted our insurance carrier.

The 2nd night, September 9, our insurance company was only able to find a hotel for us in San Bruno. That was just too far away, our son, who had been assigned a hotel in Rohnert Park, told us we could stay with him. His mother-in-law lives in Rohnert Park, so my daughter-in-law took one of our granddaughters and went and stayed with her mother. We stayed with Evan, one of our granddaughters and the dogs. That night I received a message from my daughter Taylor. She had been contacted by someone introducing their self as a photographer. They were asking if anyone had any photos of their family standing in front of their home before it burnt. They said they were writing a book. This was terribly distressing to my daughter and I became particularly agitated by the thought of someone doing this, while our homes were still burning, people were dying and missing, and evacuations were still the top priority. I also was angered that this person did not mention that they would donate one cent to anyone impacted by the fire. I knew a book was inevitable, but I was angered that someone, who obviously had not lost their home, could be so insensitive. That night I also saw a video that had been posted by a neighbor who was a fireman that lived on Aptos Court. He was recording as he drove. It became so hot at one point he stopped his vehicle. When he held his phone up again he was videoing our home. It felt like we were watching it die, it looked like it was struggling. At that point, I was so agitated that I wrote what I wanted to say to the photographer in my phone notes, just so I could get rid of the thought. It read as follows.

Profit off our loss and I'll see you in Hell. I do not want my home at 340 Pacific Heights Drive photographed. If you do I will hunt you down. Now realistically, I know people can take photos of my home, but I do not want them making money for themselves at our expense.

The following day, on October 10th, our insurance company arranged for us to stay in another hotel, but it was evacuated because of fire before we got there. They then arranged for us to stay in another hotel, but the power was out, and we couldn't use it.

The insurance company also arranged for us to get a rental car. After we picked up the car, and my husband had left to go to the office, he called and said he heard that we could go home. I was so excited. I knew our home was gone, but it was the only home I known for half my life. It was the home that we raised our four children in. Three had written their names on the subfloor before the carpet was installed. One of our children was brought home from the hospital to that house. It was the only home she had lived in until she left for college. I had just pulled out of car rental lot when Marshall called again to say that they had shut our subdivision down and no one would be allowed in. I'm not big on crying, it gives me a headache, and I'm an ugly crier, but the second I heard that we couldn't go home I began to sob. It wasn't even crying, it was sobbing. I was sobbing so hard that I knew I had to pull over. I turned down the first street and stopped on the side. After I got myself together I looked around. I had turned on to a dead-end street. The street was lined with cars, with people sitting in them. People with nowhere to go. People who may not know if they had a home. These people weren't my neighbors, but they were someone's neighbor. We all live in the same community.

Starting Tuesday until Friday our insurance company was unable to find us anywhere to stay. We were very lucky to have made friends with a wonderful family who opened their home to us. They fed us, let us sleep at their home and showed unconditional kindness. During one of the voluntary evacuation periods their area was notified. Susan packed and bag, preparing to leave if necessary. Fortunately, the evacuation did not take place. The following day Susan made me laugh when she expressed her disgust at what she had packed to evacuate. I think her list was pjs, toothbrush, and a loofa. She said the loofa was for a gift and she didn't even like them. Their home was so comfortable and familiar. I would walk through and say we had that, we had that, we had something almost like that. It was the most normal I would feel, including the months that followed.

It was about 2 weeks before our area was considered safe to enter. It's very strange to see the National Guard at your street.

I can't speak to what the fairgrounds or any of the areas set up to help people were like. We were very fortunate and opted to not go to any of those places, so people who needed them could. I worried about friends who became very quiet. I worried about people in our community that may not be "legal" but are an important part of our community.

We were very lucky, we had friends who offered homes for us to live in. We are very fortunate that we have a rental. But the idea of evicting someone, who didn't start the fire, was an impossible thought for me. I would rather sleep with my horse than evict our tenant and his family.

At night we would drive to see if the hotel we'd been assigned to had power. The trip was surreal. The posts for the barriers along the freeway were burning everywhere. There were so many other things burning that were more dangerous, that they had just allowed them to burn. They burnt for days. The Hilton was continuously burning because of gas. Then it was dark. No lights, just dark.

On Friday, October 13, our insurance company found us a hotel room in Petaluma. The traffic and commute were difficult for everyone. At one point all the gas was turned off in Santa Rosa. Around Coddingtown none of the lights were working, but it wasn't a real problem since there was no traffic to speak of.

For 12 days I tried ordering clothes online. They would be delivered somewhere, and since there was a voluntary evacuation in effect no one was home. Since it wasn't my regular address the package wouldn't be left, and I would receive a notice to pick it up at the main post office. I finally decided to give it a go. I went to the main post office and stood in line. The people working there were from other areas, because a lot of employees that worked there were afraid to leave their homes for fear the fire might turn their direction.

The post office, meaning well, told FedEx and UPS that they could leave their packages with them and they'd get them to their customers. They had no idea the volume, nor did they have the equipment to read on another's bar codes. Those of us standing in line offered to alphabetize them or put them by zip code but were told since we didn't work for the post office we couldn't deal with the packages. They said there was just a big pile in the back. Later, I heard everything was returned to FedEx and UPS and they maned warehouses in the bay area and tried to find where to deliver the stuff before returning it to the sender. I placed one order 3 times.

We finally made it to the old Press Democrat building to file for FEMA, check in with the DMV, which was amazing, and I would go to the DMV all the time if it was really like this, and other the other businesses that gathered together for one stop shopping. Right off the bat, we found out that someone had already placed a claim against our property. From what I was told FEMA loses billions of dollars to these crimes. Someone at FEMA told me that when Equifax had their data breach last year they didn't tell anyone for a couple of months, then they downplayed it. Then, a couple of months later they said it might have been a little worse than they originally thought, by July, they said it was a severe breach and offered to give you 1 whole year of free credit checking. Wow, thanks! They never did much about contacting the people whose information had been stolen, but that would be too responsible. For us, we never expected to get anything from FEMA, we gave them our information for statistics. If we hadn't we never would have known that a claim had been filed against our property.

The end of the story is, someone did submit a claim. I received a letter that looked like a forgery staying they weren't going to give us any money because they suspect fraud. The letter that looked like a fraud wasn't, but the claim was a fraud. I called FEMA again, and got the Fraud Department. They had my name and SS#, they had my husband's name and his SS#, when they said my email address they were correct, when they said my husband's email address is was something like JohnSmith@yahoo.com. Wrong. Then, they said, and your banking information is at blue dot or green dot bank. I've never heard of any dot bank, and blue or green dot is wrong. They said that when Equifax lost the social security numbers some criminals overseas ran the numbers against people's equity. The numbers that showed potential were then added to another program that alerts to any natural disasters, death, basically any opportunity they would have to get your money. The government will never get the money back. I was told to complete my case I needed to go to the FEMA office with 2 pieces of ID. My house burnt down. I don't have 2 pieces of anything. A few days later my social security card came. It doesn't have my picture, it says not to be use as identification, but FEMA said it was good enough. No wonder there is a problem.

I've been having a lot of trouble sleeping since the fire. I try to stay busy. Until it got too hot I was spending everyday just sitting on my property.

I know I've had trouble accepting where we are living. The new neighbors have been very kind and welcoming, but we are not here because we want to be. One day when I was getting ready to take a shower I looked at my purse and was ready to pick it up and take it into the bathroom with me, just in case something happens. What else could possibly happen that I need to take a purse into the bathroom. My purse usually sat in my car and I didn't even bring it into the house, now I'm ready to take it into the shower with me. I sat on the bed for a moment and decided I'd throw myself on the floor before I let myself pick the purse up. I knew there were times things would be strange, but this was over the line. I did eventually get up and take a shower without touching the purse.

I've seen tour buses go through our neighborhoods. The day they were removing the remains of our incinerated home a hot air balloon was giving a tour right over the top of us.

One weekend all our children came home. They were looking for anything that connected them to their childhood home. Just in that one day the following happened. I went to go pick something up for my family to eat. On my way back, I could see 4 strangers in my 2 doors down neighbor's home. I pulled over and waited. Since the fire I can see forever in every direction, so watching someone is not difficult. I waited until they got in their car, then I pulled up and cut them off. I rolled down my passenger window and asked if they happen to know the name of the person whose home they had been touring. They all started talking at once. Later, a car pulled up in from of another neighbor's house. There were 5 people. They didn't see me until I started to walk across the street with my phone pulled out videoing them. They got in their car and left without a word. You'd think my day would be complete at that, but no, not yet.

As the day was coming to the end, and the light becomes perfect for photography, I spot a person walking through the neighborhood, going house by house, getting just the right shot. As he photographed my next-door neighbor's home. I had my grandchildren stay where they were and walked across our lawn. I asked him if he knew the people whose home he was photographing. His answer was, "I can do whatever I want". True. I stepped closer and asked, "do you have a soul?" He asked me to repeat what I said, so I did. He again said, "I can do whatever I want". True again. I stepped closer and said "I understand you can do whatever you want, and I too can do whatever I want. How about we get some matches and go burn your house down. Then, we will both have something to take pictures of". He left. Just as well.

I try to be a good person. I try to mind my own business, and not bother other people. I try to be helpful if needed. But, if I keep getting poked things go sideways rather quickly. One of the first things I did was post No Trespassing signs on all sides of our property. The signs said no photography please. If you needed access to my property I had my phone number on the signs. Our house was quite impressive looking the rusted 3 car garage iron beam twisted, but still standing, that, along with my husband's 1966 Ford Mustang, now ruined.

I had family history I was copying for 10 family members that took up 4 huge tubs. It went back to 1503. There is telegraphs, diaries, family stories. I had a full set of chairs made of wood and leather that had started in Missouri and traveled by covered wagon across to Bend, Oregon. They even had an Indian attack that everyone survived, but they learned to circle the wagons, not the cows. Circling the cows, just made them easier to get an arrow shot in the cows. I lost photos albums that went back to the 1800's.

Marshall had brought home 2 photo albums he planned on copying for his brothers and sister.

Everything is gone. The things that mattered the most can't be replaced. I especially felt terrible for Evan. Everything in his home is gone. Everything of his at our home is gone. It's like the first 26 years of his life were erased. I kept everything my children wrote. All their drawings, gone. Instead of fancy art in our home we had things our children had done professionally mounted and hung. We had kept all their toys and brought them out when our grandchildren came over.

After they cleared the lot I thought I'd feel better, but there was no sign that we had existed. No sign of all the parties we had, all the holidays, and the ups and downs of raising 4 kids. The place where my grandparents had celebrated their Christmas Eve anniversary, where my friend celebrated her Christmas Eve birthday. Those people are all dead and gone now. I always thought I would die there. There are still times I wish I hadn't woken up. I had a full life.

We will get through this, we are going to rebuild, but I'm not sure I will die in this new home. We are making plans for that, but we'll see.

It was about a month ago when I finally realized why I'm so unhappy and lonely where I am now. I'm doing more activities out of the house than before, but still feel lost when I'm here. Then I realized, it was the things we had acquired during our lives, our children's drawings, family photos, blankets my grandmothers crocheted, the plaster cast of my grandfather holding my daughters' hand, the folded military flag from my father's burial. All that is gone and will always be gone, but the stuff was like an old friend, a lot of those memories will go away as well because those things were a que.

For a while, I had been noticing my steering wheel moving when I got around 40 mph. As time went on it became more severe. I took my car in to be serviced. They assumed I would be picking it up that afternoon. Instead the shop had it for a week. They couldn't figure out what was causing the steering wheel to shake. They balanced and rotated the tires multiple times. Finally, they discovered the heat had damaged one of my tires and it was separating. The tires otherwise looked good and had about 20,000 miles on them. New tires all around.

When we had professional family photos done after Christmas, I sort of jumped the gun and ordered pictures that we would hang in our new home. When they came I considered storing them, but I'm not familiar with how dry this place really is, and I was concerned that they may get damp and mold, or mice might discover them, so I hung them where we are staying. It was so distressing to me. It made it look like it was moving in. Then, I realized I'm treating this place like a hotel. We are here but have no ties. We have no reason to decorate or settle in. As soon as we can leave we will.

For my husband he has his work, so his mind is taken away from the situation during the day. For me, I never get away from it. I horseback ride and feel better, then I come back here. I do Pilates and feel better, then again, I come back here.

After Katrina we went to New Orleans and volunteered to help. We couldn't imagine their loss. Until we lost our home we could imagine our loss. We went back to New Orleans a couple of months ago and visited the Lower Ninth Ward. There I spoke with a woman who had lost her home during Katrina. I asked how do I move forward? She told me you never get over it, time just keeps going on with or without you.

I get tired of taking tags off of everything I want to wear. First your underwear is in a plastic bag, then you have to remove the tag, then the next piece. I was going to do something, and I thought I should wear some old clothes I don't care about. Everything I own is the same age. I could wear anything in my closet and it would be the same.

I'm sad I have nothing to leave our children or grandchildren. The family stories are going to be gone because the things that went with them are now gone. I think my kids are relieved because 2/3 of it was crap. I can agree with that, but I sure miss the 1/3.

It's just one foot in front of the other, but sometimes I trip.

Kathryn Kubota

Santa Rosa, CA

Teresa Speakman

Hi Paul... I have been so busy with animal rescue that I
haven't had time to reply unless it is a pet emergency!

I am a volunteer with Lake County Animal coalition and I am
the fire pet facilitator of the Moose Lodge evacuation center

I work hands on with the fire pets and their owner's with
emergencies, supplies, transportation, foster and placements

I haven't had much rest since Friday night and today was long
and brutal and very emotionally tolling in me!

We have over 100 dogs on site, so these are my hardest and
my busiest day's and we are shorthanded on volunteers, so I
am completely drained and need to rest tonight...

I would be glad to share some of my experience of the good
and the bad and the sad when it comes to the fire pets, but it
will take me a few days to do it due to my current situation
with this fire burning at my back door and my volunteer
status... Thank you for your information

Teresa Speakman

Rachel Forbis

My grief, My journey

Unimaginable grief is something I now live with; the memories of my lost home, business, pets, neighbors, and unborn twins. I'm learning how to cope better as time passes but doesn't mean it's getting less painful. I'm just learning how to live with it and continue on because there is no other choice. I cannot change that terrible night - it was completely out of my control. It was something much bigger than us, a nightmare that nobody should have to go through.

That unforgettable night of October 9, 2017, my husband and I were woken up from our beds at 1:00 AM to my parents knocking on my door. I was alone. Our house was about 20 feet from the house on a shared 2-acre property, so we were always in contact with each other. I wondered, however, why my mom and dad were both at the door together, it felt strange at this time of night.

When I answered the door, they told me that "we are sorry to wake you up, but you might want to consider packing in case we need to evacuate. There is a fire up the hill, it's a ways away and I'm sure we will be fine. But just in case. And we are sorry to wake you."

From sticking my head outside the door, I could smell smoke. It was a very heavy smell... like putting your head right over a campfire. I was immediately concerned by the intensity of the smell... but still wasn't totally alarmed. My husband was reluctant to wake up, as he had to get up for work in just a few hours. I told him, "no, really, we should consider packing." We decided that we would wake up our two-year-old daughter from her crib if we absolutely had to, but to wait it out and see what was actually happening.

I started pacing in circles, half awake, feeling overwhelmed, yet frozen at the same time. I didn't know what to do. After throwing on some clothes, I put my wedding ring on that happened to be in my bedside table. I take it off the day before because I thought the prongs were loose and I didn't want to risk losing my grandmother's diamond. I snatched the food container from the kitchen and poured in my favorite costume jewelry. At the same time, my husband grabs some protein bars and a box of cereal, along with a few of his favorite T-shirts. I briskly walked upstairs to my office where I snatched my laptop. I take a moment to stare at all of my treasured paintings from over the years, art supplies, thousands of dollars in inventory stored in the room for my personal design business. I just got my office perfectly organized just a week prior and prided myself on my investment supplies that I was going to be using for my client projects. I thought to myself, "I need to find a large box and fill it with all of my oil paints... I'll come back for them."

I proceeded to go back downstairs and into my parents' house. My mom, dad, and husband at that moment were frozen in front of the TV, flipping through these channels and looking for anything related to a fire. But there was nothing, they immediately split up and went their separate ways. Feeling a sense of urgency, I started moving faster. I rush past them and went outside, throwing my precious few items in the car. I became immediately overwhelmed by the intensity of the smoke, that was suddenly swirling around my body. It felt like I was in a windstorm of smoke and heat. I noticed my daughter was in the backseat of my car at this point, half-awake from my husband rushing her into the car seat. Suddenly from somewhere outside. My husband yelled at the top of his lungs, "it's here, the fire is here!"

At that point I knew the wildfire was upon our home, plummeting fiercely down the hill towards us. I never looked directly at it, but I could feel it. I was in such a state of urgency at that point that I ran to my house one last time, focused on the task at hand. I had to grab my photo albums and car keys. I ran to my daughter's bedroom, grabbing a stack of handmade photo albums. The bedroom seemed to be filling the smoke and the power was going out as the ceiling lights were blinking.

I was inhaling toxic black smoke, unable to breathe. As I tried to sprint out of the house, many of the photo albums fell from my arms. They were too heavy and at that point it was life or death, so they were left behind. I snatched up my car keys that were resting right by my front door. Thank God, they were sitting there.

As soon as I jumped into my car; sparks, embers and fire itself was raining down on the windshield. I laid on the horn in a panic to announce that I was leaving. I had no idea where my husband was. A few seconds later, he jumped into the car and we whisked away – blindly steering down our long, curved driveway. I couldn't see a thing in front of us.

We were engulfed in a sea of smoke. I focused on where the road should be and kept going. As we sped past my neighbor's car, I just drove through the flames. It was the only road out. At the time, not realizing our neighbors were still in their driveway.

As soon as we got onto a main road, we passed Cardinal Newman Highschool. I sped through the intersection that had embers and what looked like tumbleweeds on fire just blowing through it. We passed Willis Wine bar and immediately hit gridlock traffic.

At this point I started screaming. I thought we were going to burn up right there in our car, as we had nowhere else to go. I glanced at the dashboard. It was 1:20 am. We had woken up at 1:00 am. So, all of this had happened in a blur of just 20 minutes. In that short period of time, the firestorm had traveled like a freight train over the hill, wiping out everything in its path. Utter shock is an understatement for this unbelievable reality.

During that time, my parents had gotten their horse loaded into the horse trailer, but also sped off as the fire approached. They ran out of time as the trailer was not properly attached so they had to drag it out. My mom drove her van and my dad in his truck with the horse and trailer. They got in a car accident with each other on the way out from the lack of visibility. But made it out shortly after us. My severely disabled brother lives in a group home down the street from us. We were worried about him but found out that he was evacuated before us.

All of us were able to eventually retreat to Ft. Bragg where we lived in a Motel 6 for the week while the fires still raged back at home. We knew our house was gone, we knew it because we almost died. A friend who works for the fire department went to check on our home. He sent us a picture. I will never get that image out of my head. It looked like an atomic bomb went off. My home of 30 years and everything I own absolutely destroyed. Seeing the photo made all the emotions much more real, the awareness the we had been there in those final moments.

We found out just a few days later that our next-door neighbors and family friends of 30 years did not make it out that night. A wonderful older couple, who could not outrun the evil storm. All we can do is pray that they weren't in pain, that they were taken quickly. It's unimaginable and my heart goes out to them and their children and grandchildren.

That night was horrific and the weeks that followed were immensely difficult. Every morning I would wake up in a hotel and realize that everything that happened was a reality and not a dream. We were finally allowed to go back to the property a few weeks later.

Before hand, I walked into a Goodwill Thrift store because I had to buy our family shoes that could wear while we walked and sifted through the rubble that used to be our home. When I got to the checkout counter, paying for 4 pairs of sneakers, the lady tells me it will be $50 for the shoes. I asked her if they could do anything for fire survivors, and she said no. A woman in line behind me pulled out $100 and handed it to the cashier. I turned to her to thank her, then uncontrollably burst out into tears. I came to the realization that I no longer owned sneakers and was overwhelmed by her generosity. She gave me a huge hug and told me "good luck to you and your family".

We were interviewed by NBC Bay Area News that week, and our story aired the next evening. Our family spoke about how we escaped the fire, and our relationship with our deceased neighbors. It was surreal to be that person on the news. You hear of terrible stories every day, and never think it's actually going to happen to you.

About two weeks after the fire, I found out that I was pregnant with twins. The timing was quite crazy, but my husband and I were ecstatic. I can't believe we evacuated that night and I was pregnant with twins and didn't know it. We felt like, after such a horrific loss, these babies were going to be our "double rainbow" as they say. After every storm come a rainbow. We felt that we could look toward the future and have that excitement to focus on.

 I applied to a local organization, G&C Autobody and the Crozat Family Foundation to see if I could get a vehicle to accommodate our growing family. Needless to say, our prayers were answered, and we were surprised with a minivan. We were presented with it while being aired on KZST Radio. We were in total shock over the generosity and it warms our hearts beyond words. We live in a wonderful community of people who have been so giving an wanting to help our family, we truly feel blessed.

Well, a few months later, when I was 5 months pregnant, I lost both my twin boys due to severe pregnancy complications. It was just too much loss in a short period of time to bear. I sunk into a depression, really re-living the fire at that point because my future with my boys was destroyed. It's been a roller coaster of emotions to say the least, with horrible things happening to the point where you feel like "why is this happening, how can this all happen to us?"

But we've also been lifted up by our community in Sonoma County and people around us that really care. We have so many stories about volunteers that have helped us and strangers that have lent a hand. It's those people, friends, and the family that have gotten me to where I am today.

I don't believe that everything happens for a reason. There is no reason for all of this. But, I can say that I survived, we survived, and I am a stronger person now. I have my family, and we are survivors.

I now live by the quote, "you never realize how strong you are until being strong is the only choice you have."

With all my heart, Rachel Forbis

Jack & Debbie (Edens) Wright

LOCATION: Santa Rosa/Larkfield. Cardinal Newman High School. Behind the football field/tennis courts

on Angela Drive.

The Tubbs Fire erased 223 accumulative years of family treasures, and identities through personal

collections. Every 'thing' meaningful, familiar, and comfortable turned to dust. Far worse, death. Our

world upside down. The climb back has been insurmountable emotionally and physically. However,

when the Angels of human kindness, compassion, support, and love enter the equation our spirits soar

and our hearts cry tears of gratitude.

The life we had known for 35 years was in a magical location of rural convenience. The massive blow torch swept across our 2-acre property wiping out our home, cottage, offices and outbuildings. Our

beloved neighbors Leroy and Donna perished in the disaster as well as an unknown person by our

mailbox. With perhaps 30 seconds to spare, we barely managed to save our horse (Blue), our dog

(Libby) and family. Pretty much all else was lost.

Our son Scott, who is severely disabled, lives in a group home just 2 miles north of our home in Larkfield.

We called staff and were told that the fire department called, and they were going to evacuate all the

clients.

Smoke was not that uncommon with wood burners and fire pits being used in our area, so I was not all

that concerned when I moved Blue to her back paddock and smelled smoke. A window was open, and

we were aware of the smoke that seemed to get worse. My husband and I searched the internet with

Cal Fire and learned there was a fire in Calistoga, some 20 miles from our home.

Then we saw that there was fire at Safari West, which is only around 10 miles from us. I didn't put the

two fires together. In our area I hadn't noticed the wind, nor had I seen or heard the news about the

weather conditions. We eventually decided to drive and see if there was anything more we could learn.

We hit a roadblock just 1-mile up Mark West Road set up by sheriffs, advising us they were evacuating

the area, and no one was allowed in.

We turned around and stopped at Bad Ass Coffee where people were mingling. They were mostly

employees of Safari West and were concerned they were not allowed in to help with the

animals. At that time, we decided to head home and wake up our daughter, and her family (Rachel, Jake

& Sophia Forbis). We did not feel the fire would reach our place, but we wanted to remain alert.

I walked through all the rooms in our home and between denial and disbelief, I grabbed nothing.

"Where does one even begin," I told myself. In our upstairs office, I started going through drawers and

heard Jack scream "Debbie, we have to leave now!" The reality still had not sunk in, for we were just out and saw no glow in the sky. Then suddenly, I heard the deafening freight train sound of the roaring fire

bearing down. Jack screamed again with a new heightened sound of urgency, "DEBBIE WE HAVE TO GET

OUT RIGHT NOW!!!"

Panicked, I grabbed our emergency money and computer and ran down the stairs to a fire tornado

swirling beside my car. Frantically, I sat the bag down on the road to load my computer and in a state of

frenzy I left the bag with our $5000 emergency cash along with other important papers.

Running at full speed I gathered my horse but couldn't disconnect the chain from the gate, my hands

were shaking and paralyzed. This simple task suddenly became impossible. I had 2 choices, either

abandon my horse and climb over the fence or get my head together. Thank God Blue was calm and

trusted me.

The fire was upon us but strangely I couldn't look at it, my mind or time wouldn't allow it, I guess. Rachel experienced the same phenomena, ironically. Or is it ironic? There was not a second to

spare. I couldn't' breath, it felt like I was going to succumb to the smoke as I loaded blue into the trailer.

I remember thinking, "we are all going to die!"

In all the distractions and terror, Jack thought I hooked up the horse trailer and I thought he had. We

did not remove the wheel chocks from the trailer, nor did we securely lock the trailer to the ball hitch on

the truck. Fortunately, we did connect the 2 chains to the truck. Jack heavily accelerated but neither

the truck nor the trailer would budge, and fire was falling. With the pedal-to-the-metal the 1-ton truck

finally pulled the trailer over the chalks.

Suddenly, the front of the trailer dislodged from the ball hitch and crashed to the ground with Blue,

making our escape even more harrowing. Jack could not get out and investigate at this stage, fire was

everywhere. So, he again heavily accelerated dragging the trailer through the dirt, up onto the driveway

and down our road to safety. It was only connected by the 2 safety chains. One attachment of those chains had opened and stretched out nearly causing one chain to fail.

In our desperation to flee the flames, I was leading us the best I could with no visibility down the road.

There were flames on both sides of us, trees were lit up as well as the fields surrounding us. I ran off the

road several times due to zero visibility running over bushes on fire and even hitting a tree. Jack could

only follow my taillights. At the end of Angela Drive I stopped momentarily to decide where to go next.

Jack slammed into the back of our van with the truck. He then pulled around me to lead the way to

Kaiser Hospital parking lot which was about 2 miles from our home. I followed the horse trailer

dramatically swerving from side-to-side and leaving sparks flying in its wake. We parked the truck and

trailer and began the search for our son Scott.

We had gotten word that his home had burned down so we attempted to head north on Hwy. 101 to his

home. About ½ mile up 101, a 30' wall of fire crossed the 6-lane highway just in front of us. This is where the fire took out Kmart and Coffee Park in Santa Rosa. We all slammed on our brakes and turned

around heading southbound in the northbound lanes. We received a call not much later from staff at

Scott's home letting us know he was safe and where he was now located. This was not too far from

Coffee Park it turned out.

After loading Scott and his wheelchair in our van, we attempted to head back to Kaiser to rescue Blue.

There were roadblocks and sheriffs telling us we could not enter that area. We yelled out "sorry but we

have to get our horse!" They yelled back "go, go, go." We were the only people heading back towards

the fire area.

When we arrived at the Kaiser parking lot, our next-door neighbor Ken was there keeping an eye on our

horse. Jack had notified him of the plan. I unloaded Blue and after several attempts and giving it all they

had, they finally lifted the front of the trailer to the truck ball and we were on our way.

Now it was a matter of getting out of traffic jam in all directions with unbearable smoke. There is

nothing like sitting still and knowing there is a firestorm approaching you from behind with no escape.

Rules on the road when desperate goes out the window but in this jam up there was a lot of order and

considerate drivers.

The plan with Rachel and her family was to meet in Cloverdale at my sister Gina's house. We headed west out of the fire zone and then north towards Cloverdale. As we headed north, it appeared the complete mountain range from Santa Rosa north was on fire, the sky was lit up everywhere. We felt we may not get to Cloverdale due to highway closure but finally made it there around 5am. (In all my travels that night I only had one shoe on because after loading Blue I ran so fast it fell off and there was no time to retrieve it.) The cell towers had all burned down so we could not get in touch with Rachel who was very worried. Everyone was unsure of how the others were doing.

All in all, we lost Rachel's wonderful cat "Pancake" and our chickens, who were more pets than chickens being hand raised. We were able to save ourselves, Libby, and Blue. I feel very fortunate for that.

During our recovery, Rachel found out she was pregnant, two weeks after the fire. They were identical twin boys. After 5 months, it was discovered that there were serious complications and she lost both of her babies, our grandsons. Scotty was in and out of the hospital with life threatening pneumonia and his intense care consumed us. Yes, life was filled with anxiety and at times unbearable. I still grieve when I think of the twins, my neighbors, pets and cherished keepsakes. There are still moments of difficulty with the fragmentation of things and loved ones spread all over the county.

A variety of decisions could have dealt us a different hand. We thank God to be alive. We appreciate our family, friends, and even strangers who are Angels that lifted our spirits in their benevolent concern and sacrificial action. Forever cherished, so many beautiful giving and caring people.

Holding on does not make one strong, it is in the letting go where we gather our strength. We must cling to the spirit and not the temporal things of this world. Through faith, hope, and love we will continue to find our way as I pray for all the afflicted.

Jack & Debbie (Edens) Wright

6/25/18

Austin Blystone

My recap of the fire on October 8. Me and my kids just came back from Chico California I didn't personally know there was a fire it was just any other night getting ready for work and school the next day and around 230 in the morning my mother called and before I even open my eyes my senses kicked in and I could smell the smoke and hear sirens everywhere.

I thought my house was on fire personally. As I was running outside to see what was going on there was chunks of ashes in debris falling all over our apartments. Still on fire my mother said she had to evacuate and it would be best if me and my kids did too she told me as I was leaving our apartment my cousin lives up the street I had to go over there to see if he was OK. He lives on airway behind the Kmart - the old Kmart and that's when I realized the town was burning down.

That video you seen my son AJ started recording his name is Austin Jr.. And my other son Robert was with us they were recording the trails in trailer park that's been there for over 50 years right next to the round barn burned after that we had no power for about two weeks...........there's anything else you want to know let me know

Thank you ....

Austin Blystone

Ps. we live on range and Russell av and that was the first time I thought we might actually die in a fire.

 I was just trying keep my composure and not to scare my kids more than what they already were.

We weren't affected compared to homes lost or even those lives that were lost R.I.P

Ronnie Duvall

Hello Paul,

 Glad to see yet another book being written as the story needs to be told.

Jun 10th, 2:22pm

Paul

Do you have a story to send in? I wanted to give the victims a chance to tell the story instead of all the fiction out there.

Ronnie Duvall

I believe I have a story of nonfiction. I used to live there 7 years prior to the wildfires.

When the fires struck I volunteered for the Red Cross 63 days straight to serve my community.

I am the very reason all the Christmas lights were hung, the Christmas party was held, gave away all the Christmas trees, did two NYE ball lowering's (9pm for the kids and 12 for the adults), and now I'm a project superintendent for the rebuild in CP.

I lost a house as well, just wasn't in CP.

Sadly, every disaster or event has many with the fictional stories to tell.

Brian Jeffery to Northern California Firestorm Update

May 9 ·

Wow 7 Months have passed!

I wanted to share some thoughts from the perspective of a Lumber and Building Materials Sales Person!

Last year we saw more natural disasters here as well as abroad than I have ever seen in my life!

Lumber and Building Material prices are on the rise, lead times are being extended, Material shortages are beginning!

We understand your frustration, and we to are frustrated, we want to fulfill your order as much as you want it filled, sometimes that's not going to be possible to happen quickly as you or I wish it would.

Every Home Owner should review their Home Insurance at a minimum of once every year, or when there is a relatively significant rise in the cost of real estate.

Stay Sonoma Strong, Santa Rosa Proud!!!

Together we will Rise Better Together!!!

It's going to be a long process

Inger Johanne Simonsen

To: Paul Holbrook

Subject: Re: Wildfires and Journeys End/Priest Morgan brought me a miracle

I was told that you are looking for stories from the Napa Wildfires and here is a short version of mine. There seems to be healing in the recounting so here goes:

The strong winds that had started up Sunday night were increasing in strength as I finally fell asleep around midnight. During the next couple of hours, I kept waking up because of the winds. And I noted that the electricity was out as well as a strange smell. Like something was burning. But I was too woozy to investigate. I could hear a cacophony of sirens that seemed to come from Kaiser Hospital nearby, but all I wanted to do was sleep. So, instead of investigating, I buried my head under my pillows. But then, there was a knock on my door and bewildered, I stumble to see who on earth was there.

"Mom", my son shouted, "get dressed and get in the car NOW!"

Still woozy, I grabbed a flashlight and threw on a pair of pants and a T-shirt. I grabbed my purse and hurried to the car parked by my front porch, my son impatiently waiting outside the car and my daughter-in-law at the wheel. "We are taking your neighbor", he informed me, "so we have to wait a minute".

By then, I was beginning to grasp that there was danger and the danger was fire. The air was thick with foul smelling smoke. I could hear sirens and wondered if my special friend, Priest Morgan, was OK. Since his home was even closer to the hospital and sirens, I felt sure that he must be awake.

My 84-year-old neighbor, Louise Smith, joined us, still in her jammies and a pink bathrobe. "Hurry, hurry!" Louise was fighting back tears. She had seen my son pull up, not being able to sleep, and called out to him, "take me with you".

Nearing the entrance to Journeys End where we all lived, I saw huge flames licking against the night sky. Where the hedge that separated the park from the main street was, and one of the homes in the park was on fire. It was unreal. My daughter-in-law navigated the car out of the park, past fire engines and a few cars partially blocking the route, to escape. Louise made a whimpering sound next to me. Then, we were on the road and we have been on the road for three weeks to the day now.

A few minutes out of the park, we encountered a car engulfed in flames on the 101 and the nightmare became real. We kept driving, looking for a hotel for the night thinking we could return the next day. It was 2:30 – 3:00 am but it was bumper to bumper traffic most of the time. All the hotels and motels were full. We drove all the way to San Francisco before we finally could settle down. We were worried about Louise, who would need her medication in the morning, but the old lady was holing up remarkably well.

The minute we entered the hotel room, we turned on the TV. Breaking News! Journeys End was featured. Everything was gone they said. Burned to the ground they said. Louise began to softly cry. I was too stunned to cry, then. In the coming weeks, I would do a lot of crying. We all did.

"Could this really be true," I thought." Is this all I have left in the world: the clothes on my back and my purse?" As if reading my thoughts, I heard my son say, "I am not accepting this until I see it with my own eyes". He had 9 years of animation work on a computer in his home. I can't imagine how he felt at the thought of it all being lost. Plus, they had left their three cats behind.

My daughter-in-law, choking, said, "I can't go back. I can't look at it." "I will come with you", I said. I had only lived at the park for a couple of years, but it was my retirement doll's house filled with memories from the old country, a life fully lived, baby pictures and my computer.

"I want to come too". Louise seemed surprisingly fit. "I've lived in that park for 37 years. Longer than anybody", she said. "I need to go with you".

Getting back to the park area was not easy. My son had to navigate a lot of roadblocks before we could finally park in the Kaiser parking lot. As we neared the park from the hospital side, I caught my breath:

"My house is standing!" I shouted it. I started tearing up, wondering how on earth that was possible when everything around us was destroyed. Our entire community gone. We were able to get inside the park and could see for ourselves that our street was damaged, but, by some miracle, not much.

We did not think about toxic fumes that morning, the important thing was to be able to collect a few important items from our homes, like money, important papers, change of clothing, etc. Our homes were standing, but everything around them were burned. My heart ached for neighbors and friends who had lost everything.

Priest Morgan joined us, and we were so happy to see him. The go-to guy in the park, always willing to lend a hand. And then we learned that thanks to him, our homes were still standing. And, thanks to Priest Morgan, the lady up the street, who was in a wheel chair was safely with her family. Priest Morgan had been instrumental in creating the miracle on my street.

In the next few weeks, many would praise this wonderful man for his tenacity and bravery during the burning of our community. He is a hero but insists that doing what is right does not make him a hero. He insists that he was helped by a neighbor's son, Steve, who should also be thanked because he was the one who said he heard a dog barking. When they went to investigate, they discovered the woman in the wheel chair who had been left behind and unable to help herself.

Priest has problems sleeping now, because of it. We all have problems sleeping, even though our wildfire experiences are less traumatic. We rely on rely on friends and FEMA, and I, for one, have to fight with my insurance company. I am glad that my home didn't burn. I could get important papers out of there before everything was closed down behind the big fence. But is does complicate things….

My story, part of it anyway, is really a big thank you to Priest Morgan. I will always remember the smoky morning when, by some miracle, I saw my home standing in the middle of unfathomable destruction. Prayers answered.

Inger Johanne Simonsen

Alana J. Arballo-Palter

Rising from the Ashes

6-9-18

(Santa Rosa call to Los Angeles)

Oct. 8, 2017

(The phone call) – Messenger chat

Received a facetime messenger chat from NY son Joshua around 8:30 to 9ish pm (Joshua age 15)

"Hi, mom, how are you?"

I'm good, baby boy, and you?"

"Mom, I'm worried, something is not right."

"What do you mean? Are you guys ok?"

"Mom, it's super windy. It's really hot. Look, mom, look at all your birdhouses and wind chimes blowing like crazy. I'm really worried. Mom, something is really weird about tonight."

"Joshua, honey, it's ok, it is after all fall time and the weather is changing."

"I don't know, mom. Something weird about tonight and it's super weird."

"Don't worry, Joshua, you will be ok."

"OK, mom, I miss you and I love you. Dad misses you too".

"OK, I love you too. Good night, baby boy".

"Night, mom."

Oct. 9, 2017

My phone rings (normal ring, not messenger)

Santa Rosa call to Los Angeles Playa Vista

I received the call that woke me out of a complete deep sleep. I had only been asleep for around 2 hours due to the fact that I was in Los Angeles visiting with my mom, brother, and his wife.

"Mom, we have to go, we have to evacuate!!!"

"Wait, what are you talking about?"

Mom, there is a fire, a big fire coming down our street. A lady is going around banging on all our doors and telling us to get out!! Mom, we need to leave, what do I do, mom?"

I practically fell out of bed and ran out of the guest room door. I feel like I'm running in slow motion around the kitchen, through the living room, up the stairs, tripping upwards to wake up my family.

"Joshua! Get the cat and the bird food and water! Yes, get water!" That's the only thing I could think of to tell my son to grab.

My family is watching me talk to my son on the phone. It's all they could do. I was trying so hard to remain calm, it's all I could do. I felt sick to my stomach, dizzy, like stuck in a bad dream. I was scared!

"OK, mom. I'm going to put the bird in her carrier and the cat in hers and I got all the food."

I could hear him throw the items in a bag as we were on the phone together.

"Mom, I need to go now. We need to go!"

"Put dad on the phone, I love you!"

"I love you, too, Mom".

"Babe? Please take care of you guys."

"I will, Babe, I love you. We have to go now!"

"OK, bye."

I completely burst into tears. "Dear God! Dear God! Be with them, dear God!" After I hung up, I lost it.

My mom was so tired – we all were. They reassured me, "It's OK, they got this". I left my family upstairs and went back downstairs to be all alone and drown in my fear of the unknown.

"Dear, God! I'm going to lose my home! Dear God, dear God, please make it stop! Dear God, please be with Joshua and Alberto. Dear God, please hear me!"

I go onto Facebook and there on my page I see a video of Hell on Earth! A fire coming near Kaiser Hospital. I walk home from Kaiser!!! It's that close! I go onto Facebook live and start panicking. I get in touch with only one friend and she prays for us. My friend, Karen, who lives out of state.

(Phone rings)

"Mom, we are stuck in traffic!"

"Where are you guys going?"

"We are going to Stacy's house. Mom, my phone is about to die, it's not charged. I have to go."

"OK, son, please be safe."

"OK, mom, I will. I love you."

I cried myself to sleep, I was exhausted, helpless, empty, and scared.

Early morning 6 or 7 am (Phone rings)

It's my husband.

"Babe, we are ok. We are all at Stacy's house. Babe, my job is gone. It's all gone!"

The Equus steakhouse in Fountain Grove. They are all at a coworker's home.

(Back Track) …. The chefs house. My husband knew something didn't feel right when he left the restaurant around 10:30 pm. The wind was hot, eerie and silent. Just weird.

Little did he know the beautiful Round Barn next door and Equus would never be there again when he woke up. It was his last time cooking in the beautiful Equus kitchen.

I told him, "I'm so sorry!" I cried, and told him, "I'm so sorry." I have never heard my husband sound so empty and sad. He was crushed, all the cooks and chef were!

I was to fly into Santa Rosa on Oct. 10th. Every single flight was canceled! It took me 3 days to get back home to my precious family (son, husband, and pets).

(Back Track)

Went to LAX. Crying, dropping my suitcases and loosing myself. I told them all I'm from Santa Rosa and I'm trying to get back home to my husband and son. I begged to be rerouted into San Francisco after continuous cancelled flights.

Virgin America took me home to San Francisco waive luggage fees and flew me home first class for free.

Made it to Santa Rosa airport on Oct. 13. Reunited with my husband, son and pets. Our home was saved by the grace of God but yet, I felt sad and guilty that other were not so lucky.

I work at a local pet store in Santa Rosa CA. Nothing could prepare me for what I had to walk into when I went back to work. So many of my pet Parents had lost their pets that night. So many I can't even count. All I could do was hug and cry for days. So many of my wonderful customers have vanished since this dreaded fire. I pray for everyone! Our store had no animals either, they were all safely evacuated.

Please take what you need out of my story and leave the rest behind. I finally did it. Thank you for letting me share it. Sorry for my messy writing and misspelled words.

Sincerely,

Alana J. Arballo-Palter

(Back track)

Santa Rosa CA – my home since 1981. Joshua's home since birth. Husbands home since middle 90s. While stuck in traffic, Husband and son looked back towards the entire red glow in the sky. My Husband told Joshua the next day: for sure, my job is gone.

As a result of the fires, my entire family, my husband, my child and I, received 3 separate letters terminating all three of our Sutter Health insurances as well! This fire was devastating for so many in different ways. We have recovered and all 3 of us again are safely insured. The Flamingo Resort hired my husband within 2 weeks of the Tubbs Fire.

My son is my one true hero in remaining calm the best way he could. He was the one that heard the lady at the front door, the one who was able to keep things positive and be there for his Dad while I couldn't be there. He was a kind friend and gave hugs to Stacy (the chef at the Equus).

I would like to thank Stacy for opening her home to my husband, son, our cat Suzy Q, and our bird, Sopi. We are forever grateful. Through all the tears and sadness, we have made it. One day, at a time, but have never forgot that dreadful night. Through time, I pray, we will be able to let go of the worries and stress of what Oct. 9, 2017 brought us. Through every sorrow we go through in life, it will bring new rays of hope – one day at a time.

Alana Arballo-Palter

Cadence Moeller

I am not sure if I told you this before but I met a woman at
the hopper Starbucks I work at before the fires happened(I
still work there) but I ended up meeting her because I found
out her hearing dog had passed away and I just felt for her,
my heart hurt right along with hers. We remained friends and
our friendship grew stronger. After the fires I didn't see her
for the longest time after I started working again and then
FINALLY she came in!!!! By this time, she had gotten a new
hearing dog, I was SO happy to see that she was ok!!! She
told me something that I hadn't known before.... she had
lived in a mobile home park, it was called journeys end....... I
was so surprised, and I asked her how she was ok, and I was
so thankful! She told me that she had woken up and her
house was actually on fire and her dog was crated, which if
she hadn't been crated, she probably would have alerted her
to the danger, but her being deaf, she couldn't hear anything.
She literally escaped with the clothes she had on and her

dog, they got into their car and drove not being able to see anything. I love this little lady, she has the heart and soul of a lion, a warrior. (I am not sure if your able to publish this.... but I just wanted to tell the story) thank you and I look so forward to the book.

Robin Baum

I'm crying as I write this. A year ago, last night I never went to sleep. Around 9:45 pm I heard about 2 fires on either side of the freeway in Windsor and I was worried because it was so windy. I called my mom and warned her to be ready to evacuate, then I turned on Broadcastify. I listened in horror as I kept hearing about fire after fire. Atlas, Partrick, Tubbs, Pocket. I worried one of those would head up to my daughter's in Hidden Valley Lake, never even considering one would come the other way and could soon reach us.

Between 11:30 and 3:00, I woke up my husband and son to start packing, got my mom over to our house, we filled up our cars, and started waking our neighbors. Then we waited. Cable out, power out, no radio available, I continued to listen to Broadcastify because I wasn't sure which way to go.

I could see a glow to all sides of us except west. Fortunately, we were safe and only had to evacuate once briefly a few days later. But I still cry. We didn't lose our house, but I lost a big part of my childhood home - Santa Rosa. My older kids lost the house they grew up part-time in with their father.

My job-site was closed for almost a month, so I had to work elsewhere during that time. My youngest son lost his school (Anova, the school for autistic children) and they haven't been able to rebuild due to the LBC being under-insured.

I know I'm one of the lucky ones. I didn't lose my house or my job, a pet or a loved one. But I still cry. My husband and mother say I have PTSD, and I suppose I do, but I don't know why since I didn't lose everything like some others did. But I still cry. I cry when I pass the site where the Round Barn stood; I cry when I pass the corral where Angel used to stand; I even cry when I pass the stupid old K-Mart site where I used to buy my kids clothes and Christmas presents as a single mother. I cry when I look at pictures of places burning that I didn't know, and I will now never know. But I can't stop looking at the pictures...and I can't stop crying.

Lyz Wiggins

I woke up at exactly the time we were evacuating a year. I started to post photos, text messages, video footage of my frantic solo haul with my horse and livestock across our fire raged city. But I stopped.... how was one tragic night an anniversary?

You see, the Tubbs Fire didn't end in one day, and it didn't end in one week, and it certainly didn't end in a year. And it won't end any time in the future. Every day we drive to our property we used to call home, the remains of the Tubbs Fire will live on. Even after we rebuild a beautiful new home, the Tubbs Fire will live on in the loss.

The loss of neighbors, friends, homes, entire communities, and complete devastation of our rural landscape. The way we now measure regrowth is with a simple phrase, "Not in our lifetime".

And so, we push on as we deal with daily uncertainty. Once homeowners, now tenants living in strange homes with furniture we don't own, on borrowed insurance time. The battle lives on to fight for insurance clarity and to collect our claims. The fight to rebuild in a micro inflated construction market. And the internal struggle to rebuild and live in peace, where our security was shattered and tragic loss occurred.

We painfully remember this dreadful anniversary, one year later with permits & plans in hand, our ground remains unbroken. The scarred lot, dotted with blacken trees struggling to survive, will one day be home again. And we will begin our new norm, hopefully before the next 'anniversary'.

#futubbsfire #wigginsstrong #tubbsfire

Dano Wano

That's me. Struggling with what emotion I'm going to feel today. To be a positive voice in the community or to be honest. We've all felt the gamut of emotions in the last year: hope seeing rebuilding, warmth in our resiliency and compassion for families who lost it all. But waking up this morning, my first thought is- don't talk to me about Flying Cars. Or Google Cars. Or Elon Musk Hyper Tubes. Or remote surgery robots. Or any of the whiz bang Watsons that IBM pimps in NFL commercials.

Because on October 9th, 2017, a town in the richest state near the cradle of technology could not send a text message. Or an EAS test. Or a Presidential Alert. Or a Drone with a club horn.

This wasn't a nano-weapon that escaped the lab. Or a Neutron Missile we'd never seen before. This was a freaking wildfire. You know, the kind of stuff that was scary in 1859? A wildfire. And the best we could do was ask our heroes in Police and Fire to go freaking door to door like they're selling vacuums in 1961. Oops, sorry there was also "reverse 911", and all 11 people probably got that call from William Shatner himself.

As you can guess, the emotion I can't help but feel is still anger. People always like "err mai gawd don't hold on to anger I just let it go" ya well I don't. I work in Communication and I am not happy that people died that night because nobody in technology or government thought we needed a way to blow up their phone even when it's on silent (WHICH EXISTS AND IS NOT DIFFICULT BTW).

So don't talk to me about Flying Cars, or the future. Because 10/9/17 could have easily been October 9th 1917.

Katherine Bass

I was in Sutter Hospital on October 8th, 2017, my Mother's 82nd Birthday. I was across the street from my son and his family's apartment complex. It was an extremely frightening evacuation, the RNs that evacuated my unit were incredible. They were literally putting us on the bus as they were grabbing whatever they could that they thought would be needed. They were putting their coats and purses on as they loaded patients. Unfortunately, I CANNOT say the same about the hospital in Sebastopol. I was only there a few days. During the time I was there I was not given the majority of the time I was there. I was on an IV and only given 2 small containers of Apple Juice a day. Every time one of my Sutter Drs would come in to see me the Sebastopol Doc would either not enact the Sutter Docs orders or remand them as soon as my Doc left. I was so afraid of ending up dying there. That I managed to get released and then went back to Sutter as soon as it opened.

I was there for about 2 weeks then to a nursing home. I still have a horrible time trying to remember it. During the time in between hospitals, we were at my daughter's house in Rohnert Park, she was terrified because she walked into the room I was staying in and thought I was dead because I was grey, cold to the touch, and barely breathing. Yeah, the whole thing was horrific.

Claire Ossenbeck

Hello Fire Survivors. I want you to know that I think of you folks that lost everything a year ago. I think of you all the time; how sad it must be and frustrating beyond belief.

We were in the unique position to have time to choose what to take as we saw the flames get closer to town. I am so sorry you had no warning. As long as I live I will not understand that. I saw the glow, the approach, felt those winds that were truly diabolical. Why weren't you warned somehow??

As the fires got closer to us over the next week, we could go back and choose what to take in the car again, what we could leave behind to fire or looters. It made me look at everything I have differently, and I feel for you. I love my possessions and sentimental keepsakes and tools and I'm so sorry you lost yours with such absolute finality.

I'm glad you're alive and I hope you're on the mend and I really hope more rains come soon to take some of the fear and loathing away from this time of year.

I know that many of us were tortured by those fires in various ways, but I am thinking of you fire survivors every day and how hard it must have been, to run for your lives, then to lose your all, your animals, your trees, your sacred spaces, your homes, and in some cases your family members and neighbors. You experienced a horror that can be described but No one would want to go there, ever.

It could have been us in your shoes, for sure. But it wasn't, and I am beyond grateful we were spared your grief and frustration. I don't take our better luck for granted, truly.

I hope people are kind to you and patient and loving. And when people are jerks, I'm sorry for that. They can't know. It's like privilege, not knowing how much better they have it simply because the pain has not happened to them. Forget them, if you can. And know that there are many of us who think of you all the time and wish it hadn't happened to you. We wish you love and healing and hope for a good resilience around your tender core. We wish blessings on you and your children and we love you and we're so very sorry this happened to you.

Brandon Bell

A letter to my wife Smilin Lacey, sharing as I've learned how not alone I am in the last year....

My sweetest Lacey Jane,

What a year it has been. It seems ages ago that I was moving into your house, so we could have a chance to build our life together. In those few short months in the house together, I felt more at home than I may have ever had.

With our castle abundant with furry rascals and us finally finding our balance in daily routine, we were on our path. Starting to paint the walls and make it our own, I finally was feeling like the man I knew I could be. Nights filled with dancing in the kitchen and dinners with friends, we brought new love and life into the family home. A home that you were raised in. Vineyards in the background and Sonoma stars overhead.

Then in the course of one night, seemingly a few short moments, it was ripped away, along with our two precious boys, Rasta and Pumpkin. All to be turned to ash and memories.

Thrown into an upheaval of survivalist living, and relying on the generosity of others, we made it one day at a time. Feelings of resentment, betrayal, confusion, helplessness, and hopelessness were combatted with love, understanding, humility, and self-medication on a daily basis. From the days in the post-apocalyptic trailer, to nights on your mom's floor, cruise ship cabins, and sneaking five animals into the hotel, and countless stay-overs at friends' houses until the circus wore out its welcome - we persevered one day at a time.

I found the confidence that you are the one I had been searching for. My lifelong partner that I knew I could depend on for the long haul, that I could take on anything with. That no matter how much we couldn't see our greatness in ourselves, we could see it for each other.

Days after our engagement, an actual house showed up for us. And we built a bathroom in it! You held on to me tight and supported me through my career hunt and moments of weakness and coping behaviors. You brought personal development work into our lives and showed me just how open my heart could become. You gave me more of myself than I had ever given.

One seminar after the next, during the spring and summer we experienced such growth and commitment. It was overwhelmingly difficult, wonderful and rewarding.

We made the move to the Redwoods and arranged the most magical wedding beyond my wildest imaginations. The love was insurmountable.

And now here we are, on this day last year, it is so vivid in my mind where we were, and what we were doing. Sorting through remnants and feverishly searching for Rasta and Pumpkin, while holding space that we would have a home again. I reflect on our nights of Christmas decorating a burned down Crestview neighborhood, with our new friend Julie. Our friends making the drive up to deliver clothes and hugs. Our parents being by our side. The unimaginable financial donations from hundreds of people far and wide. The nights where we almost fell apart, but something in our hearts told us to stay together and keep going.

As I emotionally prepare for the memorial tonight, I sit quietly in respect for how far we have come in a short amount of time. I hold you close to my heart wherever we are, and wherever we are headed. You are with me always and I am so proud to call you my Wife, and to have you as my partner no matter what challenges life presents us. Thank you for being the leader of my heart, and the follower of my soul.

Your Loving Husband,

Brandon Bell

Nancy OConnell

October 8 at 9:57 PM

one year ago, today... a year since the firestorm blasted through our home. An anniversary to mark on our calendar? I think not!

We as fire victims are all survivors. Some people in our mutual situation don't like that label, but I feel it to my soul. We struggle to live our lives normally every day with things we used to take for granted. I look past our fence line to Fountain Grove where news cameras have set up shop for the day and wonder if life will ever be the same. I usually embrace change, but sometimes a little familiar would go a long way.

So today I am thankful to have made it through this last year, and grateful to the strangers that helped us out of the nightmare a year ago tonight.

But for me personally, I will celebrate our small successes as they come. And remember that life can change in an instant, so I will be grateful for every day I am blessed to be alive.

Darlene Dearmond

Just returned home from our camp Club in Duncan's Mills Sunday evening. We left our trailer in our camp site as it was to be stored Monday by the camp crew. We came home a day early. Exhausted, we went to b d early as my husband had to get up very early the next morning for his first job of the day. My brother was living with us at the time.

I remember I couldn't sleep. Kept smelling smoke. I woke up my husband and said I think there is a fire because I smell smoke. He got up and went outside. It was around 11PM. He came back to bed and said that there must be a Fire somewhere in the wind is blowing very hard and maybe there is a fire in Napa.

An hour later I woke him up again and said the smoke is getting worse I cannot breathe. He was upset with me for waking him up again and said, "there's nothing wrong I have to go to work early in the morning, go back to sleep". I pulled the blankets over my head and started to play games on my phone.

Bored with that, I started scrolling through Facebook on my phone. It was around 2:30 AM. I see a post my friend shared from a friend of hers in Sebastopol. It was time stamped 2:13 AM. It said the fire has jumped the freeway and was burning at Kohls.

I immediately jumped up and again woke up my husband and told him about the post. Our bedroom was thick with smoke. We both went out into the living room and looked out our front windows. We lived at a four way stop, Santiago and Barnes Road. It was gridlock. It looked like the traffic you see at the fairgrounds after the Fourth of July celebration.

The wind was blowing so hard and large red embers were floating throughout the sky. People were running down the road in their pajamas caring small pet carriers and backpacks. I looked at my has been and asked him what is going on!?!?

I then called my friend that shared the post and she said that we needed to get out of there. I've beat down my brother's door because it was locked, and it took a minute for him to come out. He had a large fan on and sleeps with an apnea machine. He wasn't happy about being woken up, but we told him we need to leave there's a fire somewhere.

My husband told me to get in my car and go. I told him I can't I don't wanna leave you and my car will be fine it's in the garage. All I knew at the time was I needed to evacuate. At that time evacuation meant something wasn't right in the area and I would be displaced for a little bit. I went to show my husband that my car would be OK opened up the garage door and lock all the smoke started to fill the garage and my cat ran out. We couldn't get the cat to come back, so my husband had me take one of the dogs and get going in my car.

It took me 10 to 15 minutes before someone would let me back out of my driveway. Traffic was so backed up other people were trying to get out of their driveways or turn onto the same street I was on, but I thought no one let me out of my driveway - I'm not letting anyone else in.

I then called my daughter but realized I dialed the wrong number after the phone started ringing so I hung up. My phone immediately rang right back, and it was the number that I had mistakenly called. The woman on the other side of the phone asked me if I was all right. I said yes, no, I don't know, as I was crying. She asked me for my name and if it was OK for her to pray for me and I said yes. Her prayer sent a sense of calm over me and I realize we were all in this together.

At that moment I decided to let every car backing out of a driveway and every car that was trying to get onto the street, in front of me. I realized that we were all in this together. It took me one hour to get out of Coffey park. I went to my girlfriend's house and shortly thereafter we received voluntary evacuations from her place.

My daughter called me and told me that one of my grandson's father had had an accident and ended up in the Vineyards. They also lived in Coffey park. His father had had a seizure and my grandson called 911 and no one ever showed up. My grandson tried to flag down passing motorist, but no one would stop. He was smart enough to send a ping, still not sure what that is, to my daughter and so she sent me there to pick them up.

By the time I got there his seizures have stopped. I drove straight back out to the campgrounds it was about 5 AM in the morning crying the whole way wondering if the fire would chase us out to the ocean. I just couldn't understand or comprehend how was city full of cement and asphalt could catch on fire when we have fire departments and I still struggle with that. A few hours later we returned to the Coffey park area and found mass destruction like I have never witnessed before. My home was gone.

Deanna and Chris Diaz

October 9, 2017, our lives changed forever. Woken up by a phone call on my husband's phone at 1:06 am, a phone call that saved our lives. This is our story...

My husband handed me the ringing phone as he was still half asleep. I answered, and it was our family friends who live in Larkfield. They apologized for calling but he explained there was a fire going on in the hills behind them and they had been given the order to prepare to evacuate. They asked if the order was given, if they could come to our home.

As I was speaking to him, I got out of bed and went to look out my bathroom window- it faces north, and I could see a red glow from what looked like the hills to the north east of Larkfield. I could see and hear that the winds were very gusty, coming from the north east direction which also seemed to explain what looked like slightly smoky air all around. I confirmed with our friends that they could come to our home if they needed to, hung up with them and handed the phone back to my husband.

As he took his phone back, he noticed that there was a text message from the police department for whom he works. It was a call in of all off duty officers to help with fires in Larkfield and Fountain Grove. He called in and told the department he would be in asap.

My husband got up and got ready to leave to work as I got dressed and went down stairs to pull out blankets and air mattresses for our possible house guests. I also took the dog out to potty and noticed just how windy it was. The gusts of wind were very strong and there was a smell of smoke in the air. There were however no signs of any kind of fire in our area- only the glow way out on the north east hills.

As my husband left, he told me that he thought it would be a good idea if he left the garage door open just in case the power goes out. That was a very good idea because it is such a heavy door, it is near impossible to get open without two people when the power is off.

I began pulling blankets out from under the stairs and looking for pillows. It seemed like a good possibility that the power may go out due to the strong winds, so I also started pulling out the flashlights that I knew we had and went to the garage to get our camping lantern.

I went back inside, and my phone rang. It was my husband who was on the road to work. He said that I may want to pull out flashlights (which I had) he commented on how windy it was and that he could see a glow of fire on the fountain grove hills. He mentioned that just as a precaution I should go to our granny unit and make sure the renters (a husband, wife and one-year old baby girl) were awake and aware that the power may go out and that there were fires in Fountain Grove and above Larkfield.

I took the dog, and went to the granny unit, as I knocked on the door, the neighbors were up and a little nervous about the winds and the smell of smoke in the air. There were still no signs of any fires near us, so I told them what I knew and let them know that our friends may be coming over. At that point, we agreed that we would all just look for flashlights, and maybe pack a bag just in case there is a need to evacuate at some point.

I went back inside, and our 15-year-old daughter was coming out of her room saying that she could hear the winds and smell smoke. I told her about the fires in the hills, and that our friends may be coming over. I texted our friends to see if anything had changed... She texted back that they had been given the evacuation orders and they were getting ready to leave.

I told our daughter that It may be a good idea to pack a bag in case we too have to leave the house for a while- which she went to her room to do. I went into our nineteen-year-old daughters' room to wake her as well and told her what I knew and asked her to get dressed, pack a bag just in case of having to leave and that friends were on their way over. I headed to my room to pull out a suitcase.

My phone rang, and it was our niece. She was calling to ask if her family could come to our house because they were living in their aunt's house in Oakmont, and they were being told to evacuate due to fires in the hills around them. I told them that was fine and that we had another family coming too. That call made me feel pressured to hurry up and throw some things in my suitcase, so I could get back downstairs to prepare for the many houseguests we were about to receive.

I took the overnight bag that was in my suitcase to the bathroom and put in toothbrushes, toothpaste, my retainers, blow dryer, brush, comb and then put that bag in suitcase, and put in two of my shirts, socks ... I grabbed a pair of my husband's pants, socks..., and then the power went out.

I stopped packing and went to bathroom to get lighter and lit a candle. I went downstairs and lit a few candles in each of the living rooms and kitchen so there was some light. Both girls peeked their heads out and I reassured them that it was ok and to pack up a few things just in case.

I headed back upstairs to go to my room and my phone rang...

My husband was yelling into the phone that there was no time, the fires had jumped the freeway towards our home, we needed to get the pets and get in the car immediately. He said he was on the way to get us. He repeated there was no time...

As I listened to him, I yelled to the girls that they needed to get their bags, pets, and we had to get to the car NOW! The fire was coming, I grabbed my suitcase from my bedroom, picked up the dog, met the girls as they came out of their rooms- each had a bag or a suitcase, the youngest had her bearded dragon in her bag she said, the oldest had her bird in a small carry case and we headed down the stairs- there was no time to gather her seven reptiles.

As I looked out the front windows while going down the stairs, I could see cantaloupe size embers raining down into our front yard and lighting little fires in the bushes. My fear rose quite a bit at that point. I still could not see what was going on to the east of us. As we rounded the stairs, our youngest said she would grab the bird that lives in the cage in the living room as we went by. She grabbed her and held her to her chest and we all headed to the garage. We stopped to put on shoes. And I got my purse from that room too.

We went to garage and the smell of smoke was very strong. The raining embers were continuing, and the smoke was so thick that it was difficult to see into the walnut orchard that is on the south side of our property. My husband- in his patrol car was coming down the driveway with his lights on as we were putting our things in the car. He went past us and into the back-gravel driveway in front of the granny unit and turned on his sirens to warn the renters to get into their car and follow him. I do not remember hearing his sirens, but he told me he turned them on.

The girls and I got into the car with the pets and I pulled us out of the driveway and turned around to face out. My husband had pulled up in front of us facing back towards Coffey lane, he got out of his patrol car and ran to close the garage door, which took him about one minute to accomplish. The renters were pulled in behind him, but left room for me to get right behind my husband's patrol car.

As he led us down the driveway, he stopped again in front of our eastern neighbor's driveway and he got out and ran to their house to make sure they knew to get out right away. I saw they looked to be gathering things and I could see her car in the driveway. The renter got nervous while my husband was at the neighbors and tried to go around us on the driveway, but there was not enough room for him to get all the way by, so he stopped.

As my husband came back to his car, I followed him as he began leading us down the driveway. It was hard to see the road on either side due to the smoke, so I stayed as close to the patrol car as I could so that I didn't lose him or drive off the road. I saw that the neighbors wood pile just to the east of their home was up in 20-30 feet of flames, and the burn pile in their field was also on fire. There were large embers raining down on our car and I was scared for us all at that point but stayed focused on the patrol car's tail lights.

I knew there was a slight jog to the right in our driveway where the road goes over a dry creek bed coming up and I was very scared that the patrol car or I or the neighbors would be too far to the left and roll the car off the edge into the field. I noticed that my husband slowed down slightly around that area and I knew he was trying to judge where that creek was as well.

We could not see well at all, maybe six feet of visibility unless it was something nearby up in flames. There were cantaloupe size fire balls raining down through the sky. As we got to that creek I glanced for a second in the direction of another neighbor's home to the north and could tell it was totally engulfed in flames, and so was the house across Coffey lane from our driveway.

We made it to Coffey lane at our mailboxes and as we turned right, there was the neighbor from across the street on a tractor heading north towards the flames right next to our mailboxes... it was the old man that lived in the white house with the horses and the bull. I commented to the girls "what is he doing?" I was very concerned for him, but I could not stop to help him, Chris was continuing on and I did not want to lose him in the smoke and put my girls in anymore danger plus the neighbors were right behind me as well. It was obvious that we were all out of time.

I asked our daughters to call both grandparents (mine) to let them know that we were evacuating. I also asked both girls to contact the families that were on their way over to tell them it was no longer safe to head to our home for shelter and that we were evacuating. All this while I was following the patrol car down Coffey lane.

There were burning branches and downed power lines that we had to maneuver around and over on the way towards Hopper Ave. The abandoned yellow house on the east side of Coffey lane across from our mailboxes was completely up in flames, the structure on the west side was burning, small parts of the fields looked to have small fires starting. I kept telling the girls that It was going to be alright, and that we were going to make it out safe. I asked them several times if they were doing ok, and both girls remained strong and calm. They were both busy contacting people via their cell phones, which I felt was a good distraction.

Once we made it to Hopper Ave, my husband led us to the right and we were joining a lot of traffic. The time was about two am. There was a steady stream of cars going down Hopper and all the other streets of Coffey Park, but I followed my husband and trusted him to lead us to safety. When we got to Barns Road we turned left, and as it makes a turn back to the west there is a cross street that heads south towards San Miguel Rd.

We pulled over so that we could say a very difficult good bye- He told me to head either east to Sebastopol or south towards Rohnert Park. With a quick kiss goodbye and a good bye to the girls he ran back to his car and headed back north into Coffey Park to get as close to the fire as possible and begin helping residents evacuate to safety.

I was tearfully driving the rest of the way down San Miguel to Waltzer and to Piner Road where I headed south to Marlow and then to Hwy 12 to head to Rohnert Park. Our niece told us that her family went to a hotel there, so that is where I decided to head as well. I knew as I was driving away that our home was most likely burning to the ground.

I wanted to break down and cry, but I knew I had to be strong for the girls and I had to keep them safe. I was extremely worried about my husband. I got us to Rohnert Park to the hotel and got us a room.

It was so hard to stand in that lobby waiting my turn to get a room knowing that I no longer had a home to go back to. I really wanted my husband there with us, so we could support and console each other.

I was scared for his safety, I was in shock of what just transpired, and it was just me, alone in the lobby with a bunch of strangers that had to evacuate their homes too. The girls waited in the car with the pets as I got us a room.

We turned on the television to see what was going on... it was terrible. That is the first time I learned just how spread out the fires were. We put the bearded dragon in the bathtub, so he was confined, we put the birds on the handles of our suitcases, and I wrapped the dog's leash around her body like a harness so that I could take her outside.

We talked with other evacuees and our niece to comfort each other. I made sure to speak to my parents, one of which lived in a home off Waltzer Ave with his girlfriend where the fires were heading, so I was encouraging them to get out. I got a few communications from my husband that he was safe, and I told him about my dad not leaving. At some point several hours after we had evacuated, my husband made it to the home where my father lived and convinced them to get in their car and head to me at the hotel.

It was not for another 5 hours that I got to see my husband. About five in the morning when the inferno had finally stopped spreading, my husband sent me a short video of what it looked like... there was nothing left. It was still smoldering and there were still small fires burning in a heap of ash where our home used to be.

We spoke on the phone shortly as he tearfully told me, "It's all gone Dee- it is all gone." And although I was crying, I was numb; it didn't feel real, we were just standing in our home 5 hours ago, surrounded by all our memories and mementos of our lives and now it was all gone.

EPILOGUE

It has been my privilege to bring you the stories from the victims of the Tubbs fire. I hope you never have to go through a tragedy of this nature.

There are many charities that were set up to help them put their lives back together. I do not know if they are still in effect. If you are interested in donating, please email me at: aneaglesnest@msn.com and I will put you in touch with someone who can direct you.

If you were a victim of a California wildfire and would like to tell your story, contact me as well. If I receive enough stories to put together a second book, I would love to include your story, in your own words.

You can email me your story: aneaglesnest@msn.com

You can mail your handwritten or typewritten story:

Paul Holbrook
4622 Runabout Way Bradenton FL. 34203

Or, you can post your story on my Facebook page:

www.facebook.com/sonomawildfire/

With so many fires burning in California, there are a lot of people who could find it therapeutic to write down their experiences. As you can see, I will print them just as you write them.

If you are a victim of another type of tragedy, such as flood, earthquake, hurricane, volcano and would like to tell your story, send me that story as well.

As promised, a portion of the proceeds from this book will go to animal shelters in the Santa Rosa Area. These shelters went above and beyond to care for the animals that were also victims of the fire.

For news of which shelters receive money and when, like the Facebook page listed above.

Again, thank you for taking the time to relive these emotions with the victims of the Tubbs Fire. May your life be free from tragedy and may you enjoy happy days ahead.

Paul Holbrook Author

If you do not mind, please go to the book page on Amazon and leave a review. It is very much appreciated.

Made in the USA
Middletown, DE
19 January 2019